Aberdyfi: The Past

Early Welsh Way of Life in the Dyfi and Dysynni Area

ABERDOVEY FROM THE AIR.

by Hugh M. Lewis M.B.E.

dinas

By the same author:

Aberdyfi in Retrospect
Aberdyfi Legends and History
The Story of Aberdyfi
A Riverside Story
Aberdyfi: A Glimpse of the past
The Bells of Aberdyfi
Aberdyfi: Portrait of a Village
Pages of Time
Time and Tide
Aberdyfi Through My Window
Aberdyfi: A Chronicle through the Centuries

Praise for *Aberdyfi Through My Window:*
" ...most finely written... I consider that this is writing of distinctively Welsh local history at its best."
Emeritus Professor W.H. Morris-Jones

Dinas is an imprint of Y Lolfa

Published and printed in Wales
by Y Lolfa Cyf., Talybont, Ceredigion SY24 5AP
e-mail ylolfa@ylolfa.com
website www.ylolfa.com
tel. (01970) 832 304
fax 832 782
isdn 832 813

INTRODUCTION

Now that we have reached the twenty-first century, I suddenly find myself in my ninetieth year, full of precious memories of one of the most innovative centuries in history. This has surely been a time when the deeds of men have changed the world out of recognition.

I was born into a way of life that was so different that it is difficult to recognise today. It was a leisurely period when folk were not ruled by the clock, and there was time for people to stand and absorb the pleasant tempo of life. My growing-up took place against a background that was usually constant and secure, and where a sense of cohesion and community was ever-present.

Now that I have time to stand back and reflect, I can remember the great advances and many changes that have taken place over the years. These I have chronicled in several articles and books. No longer involved in public affairs, I keep my mind active by writing. I find that my life-long interest in local history, some well-established contacts, supported by an invaluable collection of photographs, have enabled me to build up a considerable body of knowledge about all aspects of local life, which regretfully is now disappearing.

The present book consists of a collection of articles relating to the Dyfi and Dysynni area.

Hugh M. Lewis M.B.E.

The Wharf area between 1840 and 1880

CONTENTS

	PAGE
THE RIVER DYFI FROM SOURCE TO SEA	9
THE ROMAN ROAD	15
BELLS OF ABERDYFI AND THE LOST LAND OF CANTRE'R GWAELOD	17
ABERDYFI CASTLE	22
THE BEAR OF AMSTERDAM	23
THE STORY OF THE ABERDYFI LIFEBOATS	25
THE STANDING STONE IN TYWYN (Y GROESFAEN)	31
THE TYWYN PIER (1876-77)	33
ABERDYFI'S MYTHICAL BEAST	35
A DEEP REMINDER OF THE PAST	37
CWM MAETHLON (HAPPY VALLEY)	39
THE MARINERS' BEACON	43
THE VILLAGE BLACKSMITH	45
ABERDYFI CEMETERY	47
EARLY FARMING ACTIVITY (By Oliver Gabriel)	53
FAR FROM HOME	56
EARLY HOME LIFE	58
EARLY VILLAGE LIFE	66
ABERDYFI WHARF AND LEISURE AREA	80
THE UNKNOWN WARRIORS	85

A PEACEFUL HAVEN

ONE OF MY
FAVOURITE
WELSH POEMS

Yng nghanol mor fy mywyd i
Y mai ynys fechan braf
Ac yno weithiau gyda'r nos
Yng nghwch fy hiraeth af
Does ond myfi a thonnau'r mor
Wyr am y Sanctaidd dir

MY
ENGLISH
TRANSLATION

A beautiful small island exists
In the centre of the sea of my life
Its magic draws me, often at night
On a journey away from all strife
Only the restless waves of the sea
Share this sacred place with me.

This short poem tells of an island of the imagination which exists in the minds of many people. It is an idyllic place which is waiting for you and you alone. It is where you can go with your thoughts, your wishes, your ideas and your longings.

It can be anywhere that you wish to make it; a wood, a street, a path, or a place where you have spent happy moments perhaps in childhood. It can create its own time and space for tranquillity and reflection.

Sometimes to get there you can travel over calm waters. At other times, when the sea of life is rough and stormy with events hard to bear, you may have to fight hard to reach your peaceful haven.

When you finally arrive all will be calm. quiet and restful. It will give you everything that you want. It is a place we all need.

Aberdyfi has provided me with a peaceful haven with all the time to reflect in the most perfect and tranquil of settings. It has its own magic which draws me. It will always be my home, a place of the imagination.

Hugh M. Lewis M.B.E.

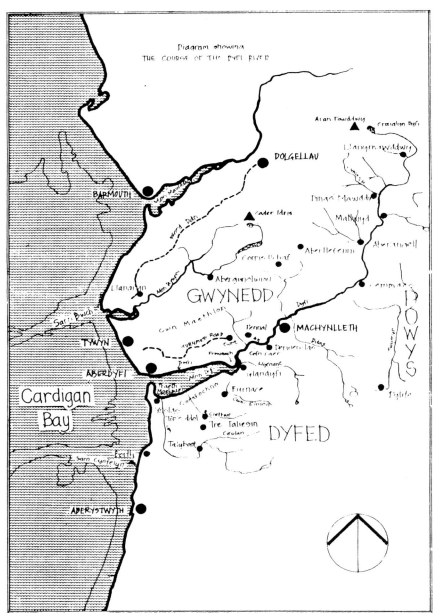

Map showing the course of the River Dyfi

THE RIVER DYFI FROM SOURCE TO SEA

The mountain range that forms the northern rim of the Dyfi basin is crowned by the second highest mountain in Wales, Aran Fawddwy (2,970 feet). Nestling under its peak lies a small but deep lake called Craiglyn Dyfi, and it is from this remote spot that the River Dyfi starts on its thirty-mile journey to the sea.

On its way, it is fed by many tiny streams and rivulets from the boggy land around. After being joined by the Rhydbwll and Gorslwyd streams, the river becomes a foaming torrent as it falls rapidly over a series of waterfalls, to the valley below. This section of the river is known as Llaithnant ('milky stream'), as from a distance the water looks white as milk.

Then the Dyfi is joined by two more small rivers, the Rhiwlech, and Pumrhyd, before reaching Llanymawddwy, a tiny hamlet dominated by the surrounding hills. Here the furious waters of the Cywarch augment the swelling river, which shortly afterwards reaches Dinas Mawddwy.

The Welsh word 'dinas' means city, and there is evidence that Dinas Mawddwy was once an important place, where the weaving of woollen fabrics and quarrying for slate were the main occupations. 'Mawddwy' means 'overflowing stream' and indicates the nature of a river, which, in periods of heavy rainfall, quickly floods the low-lying areas.

Dinas Mawddwy is 270 feet above sea level, as at this point the river has dropped considerably from its source in the mountains. Below Dinas Mawddwy, several streams feed the Dyfi, the Gerist and the Cleifion among them. The river now flows through a valley with some picturesque bridges towards Mallwyd. Then it turns westward through a deep chasm near Brigands Inn. This was named after a band of outlaws who ravaged the countryside in the middle of the sixteenth century. They were known as the Gwylltiaid Cochion Mawddwy ('the red-headed bandits of Mawddwy').

The Dyfi descends the mountain sides to the valley below

The river winds its peaceful way along the Dyfi valley

The Dyfi is now joined by the Clywedog and the Tafolog. The next village on the route is Aberangell where the River Angell joins the river, and just after the village of Glantwymyn (Cemaes Road) the Twymyn adds its contribution to the flowing river.

Still flowing westward towards the coast, the Dyfi now reaches the ancient town of Machynlleth, known to the Romans as 'Maglona'. It was here in the year 1404 that the astute Prince Owain Glyndŵr established his Parliament, the seat of government to cover the whole of Wales.

At one time Machynlleth was the centre of a flourishing woollen industry, and also some tanning was carried on. Later on, a great deal of industrial activity took place in the surrounding hills, as slate quarrying and lead mining brought some prosperity to the town. Today the wide streets are dominated by a clock tower, erected in 1873, and the town serves the mainly agricultural area of the Dyfi valley. At Machynlleth the River Dyfi is joined by the Dulas, which flows into the Dyfi valley from the Corris area.

Here the river serves as the boundary between Powys, Dyfed, and Gwynedd, as well as being the geographical dividing line between North and South Wales. The main communication is by a stone bridge, which crosses the Dyfi at Machynlleth. Built in 1805, it permits only single-file traffic across the Dyfi. From here the river is tidal and very soon becomes navigable so that, during periods of heavy rainfall, the river swells in size considerably. When it meets an in-coming tide from Cardigan Bay, the river often bursts its banks and then the Dyfi valley resembles a large lake.

Some two miles down-river from Machynlleth is the hamlet of Derwenlas, which was once a busy inland port with quays for loading and discharging goods of all kinds. It had shipbuilding yards and was the scene of much

'Pont ar Ddyfi' built in 1805 spans the river near Machynlleth

activity. There was extensive mining in this whole area.

Early in the 17th century the discovery of lead, silver, zinc and copper brought much activity to the upper reaches of the Dyfi. High up in the mountains above Machynlleth lies Dylife, where deep mining operations were started in 1720. By the year 1863 it had developed into a thriving community and had a labour force of some 700 miners. All the products from Dylife were carried to Derwenlas, a distance of some

The river widens to an estuary before meeting the open sea

thirteen miles, over roads that were little better than cart tracks.

The needs of the upper valley of the Dyfi, including the slate area of Corris and Aberllyfeni were supplied by small boats from Aberdyfi because the river provided the only highway, there being no roads worthy of the name. Limestone to supply the requirements of the farming community, as well as household goods, were brought by sea from Liverpool and London to Aberdyfi and conveyed by small boats up the river to Derwenlas for distribution inland as far as Newtown. The river boats were strongly made and required clever handling to bring them alongside the larger boats in Aberdyfi.

On a rocky plateau overlooking the river at Glandyfi we find a medieval castle. This was once the stronghold of a 12th century Welsh Prince, Rhys ap Dafydd.

Following the south bank of the River Dyfi we reach a reserve of some 600 acres which is administered by the Royal Society for the Protection of Birds, while the remainder of this area, about seven miles in length, is controlled by the National Nature Reserve. There is an area of about 400 acres of boggy land called Cors Fochno (Borth Bog) and a wildfowl refuge of 1,000 acres which in winter is the home of Greenland white-fronted geese, widgeon, pintail, mallard, teal, shoveller, shelduck, red-breasted mergansers and waders. A long stretch of sand, called Traeth Maelgwyn, reaches as far as the sea and is covered with water at high tide.

Tributaries flowing into the Dyfi from this side of the river are the Ceulan, Clettwr, Einion, Llyfnant and Leri.

From Machynlleth we follow the north bank of the river to Pennal, a Roman site. Pennal churchyard has a circular walled enclosure, which suggests Celtic church origins. In the grounds of Talgarth Park nearby there stands a huge mound believed to be the site of a medieval llys or court.

Pennal church with its circular walled enclosure around the churchyard

At Aberdyfi the river flows into Cardigan Bay

The river, as it makes its way towards the open sea, widens to an estuary. Whereas the south bank has sand banks, bogland and marshland, the north bank is in marked contrast. The steep mountain sides are covered with rough vegetation and trees growing down to the river bank.

The Dyfi has always been known as a good fishing river. Trout are to be found in its many deep pools. Salmon fishing was a common way of earning a living in the early years of the 20th Century, when several boats from Aberdyfi, manned by old sailors, regularly netted the river.

Beautifully situated on the north bank of the river is the picturesque village of Aberdyfi, a name that simply means 'Mouth of the Dyfi'. It is interesting to note that the eastern part of the village is called Penhelig. 'Helig' means an upland moorland near the sea shore, having rough vegetation, and 'Pen' means the top or head. So at Penhelig we find the beginning of the north bank of the Dyfi, whilst the village itself is on the sandy foreshore.

So ends a thirty-mile journey. It began at 3,000 feet in the mountains and culminates with the Dyfi flowing into a wide estuary and eventually into Cardigan Bay. It is a journey which began in a lake and, by twists and turns, has negotiated its way through varying features until finally it sedately and nobly reaches Aberdyfi, a dignified village which will always be proud to bear its name.

Hauling in the salmon nets, 1930

THE ROMAN ROAD

The village of Aberdyfi is of comparatively modern date, yet the Dyfi river and its surrounding countryside is steeped in legends and tales that lead one back to prehistoric times. For thousands of years primitive hunters ranged the mountain sides and sought a meagre existence on the coastal plains, but it was not until the coming of the Romans and the building of roads that the area was opened up and developed.

When the Romans subdued Wales their military occupation depended on a network of roads and forts. One of the main problems they faced was the building of the western part of the great rectangle of roads linking up Caerleon,

The old Roman road near Aberdyfi

Moridunium, Segontium and Deva. The mountains offered no easy way through and there was little opportunity along the coast. Even so, a road was built, a hundred miles in length, though little remains of it today. It went directly through the centre of Wales and was known as the Sarn Helen. Forts were built at short intervals along its whole length and one of these stood at Cefn-Caer, some six hundred yards south-east of the village of Pennal. Cefn-Caer was chosen by the Romans because it had a particular natural advantage: it stood close to a good point for fording the River Dyfi. The fort was strategically placed at the end of a low smoothly rounded spur which rises above the flood level of the river and commands the river-crossing at this point. It could also be conveniently served from the sea by way of the Dyfi river. The visible remains of the fort are today extremely scanty. Deliberate destruction and continuous cultivation of the site by generations of farmers have caused its near obliteration.

Very little is known about the route taken by the Roman Road from Cefn-Caer to Dolgellau; this is still largely a matter of personal opinion. No remains have been found between these two points, and a blank is left on most published maps. The massive bulk of Cadair Idris lies across the direct line from Pennal to Dolgellau and the Romans must have turned either east or west. There is a local tradition that the track hewn out of the rocks along the north bank of the river Dyfi on the outskirts of Aberdyfi is of Roman origin, and it has long been known as the 'Roman Road'. Beyond Aberdyfi, it is possible that the road followed the shore to Tywyn. Shifting sands along this part of the coast often reveal buried objects. For instance, an old milestone, probably of Roman origin, has been found on the beach near Tywyn. The road turned inland at the mouth of the river Dysynni to join Ffordd Ddu, a well-used mountain track running across the flanks of Cadair Idris to Dolgellau. The ancient cairns along the course of this track indicate that it is probably of prehistoric origin.

Y Domen Las (The Green Mound) in Talgarth Park, Pennal – site of a mediaeval 'Llys' (Court)

THE BELLS OF ABERDYFI
and
THE LOST LAND OF CANTRE'R GWAELOD (THE LOWLAND HUNDRED)

Aberdyfi has lent its name to one of the loveliest of Welsh ballads. How many people who have never been near Aberdyfi, or who are not even aware of the existence of the village, are familiar, perhaps from distant childhood memories, with the melody of 'The Bells of Aberdyfi'. It has the simplicity and naturalness associated with Welsh folk-song, and yet all is not what it seems.

According to *The Oxford Companion to Music* 'The Bells of Aberdyfi' is not a folk song at all, and is certainly not Welsh. It appears to be the composition of Charles Dibdin, a successful composer of musical dramas who lived from 1745 to 1814. He published the song in a volume of his compositions in 1785, and it appeared in many subsequent volumes.

But its most famous appearance comes in Dibdin's Drury Lane hit 'Liberty Hall', where it is sung by a comic Welsh character. It is hard to believe that such a well known song should have had such strange beginnings; no doubt the beauty of the melody and the sentiments of the words ultimately won 'The Bells of Aberdyfi' its place in the hearts of Welsh people.

At a later date Madam Edith Wynne, known as the 'Welsh Nightingale' nightly electrified the Drury Lane audience with her rendering of the song. As Lady Mortimer in Shakespeare's *Henry IV*, Miss Wynne had to sing a Welsh melody, and her choice was always 'The Bells of Aberdyfi'.

One of the first questions that visitors to the village ask is 'Where are the bells of Aberdyfi?' They cannot be the bells in the present Parish Church, as many people seem to think. These bells were installed as recently as the year 1937 and the church itself was only built some one hundred years earlier. For an explanation we must turn to the legends and stories associated with the old song, of which there are several different versions.

One story tells of a huge giant, Idris Gawr, who once upon a time roamed the mountainous area to the north of Aberdyfi carrying a huge bell. He used to sit in solitary splendour on the highest peak, known as Cadair Idris (The Chair of Idris). Sometimes he would descend from

CANTRE'R GWAELOD
The remains of the old boundaries
SARN Y BWCH and SARN CYNFELIN

Cantre'r Gwaelod: The remains of the old boundaries Sarn Y Bwch and Sarn Cynfelin

the mountains to wade in the River Dyfi at low water, but one day a storm blew up and he was overwhelmed by the heavy seas and drowned. The giant's bell is said to sound over the sands at certain hours and seasons.

Another more humdrum account is as follows. A peal of bells was once brought from Flanders to be placed in the Aberdyfi church tower. Before they could be landed however, the ship in which they were being carried was overtaken by a storm. The bells made the ship difficult to control and the captain showered curses on them and ordered them to be thrown overboard. The bells are still sometimes heard tolling at the bottom of the sea.

A romantic story tells of Menna, the beautiful daughter of a local farmer. He owned many sheep on the mountains around the estuary of the Dyfi and Menna was his shepherdess. She had to roam the hills in all weathers and sometimes, when looking out to sea, she thought of her lover, a young sailor who had travelled to distant lands. She soothed her longing by singing to the melodious accompaniment of the bells around the necks of her many animals as they moved restlessly from place to place. In those days, before the Roman occupation of Wales, upland farmers attempted to secure a living from the wild and mountainous terrain around Aberdyfi. The land

was open and free, and their animals were allowed to rove at will. This meant that a careful watch had to be kept on the scattered flock both by day and night, so it was customary to tie little bells around the necks of all sheep and goats, as is done in Switzerland to this day.

There is a pastoral verse, with anglicised and broken spelling in the Bodleian Library at Oxford which can be sung to the melody 'Clychau Aberdyfi'. The mention of sheep and goats on craggy mountains may well be a reference to Menna and her flock on the mountains above Aberdyfi.

From these fascinating stories and legends, based on fact, comes the well known song which is Aberdyfi's chief musical claim to fame.

Looking westwards from the slopes of the mountains above Aberdyfi, one sees the wide sweep of Cardigan Bay with the sea in its many moods. It is difficult to picture this area as a rich and fertile plain stretching far out for many miles, but it was so, and the story of 'Cantre'r Gwaelod' (The Lowland Hundred) is about the submerging of this land by the sea in the fifth century.

The Oxford Dictionary states that the old English or Saxon Hundred was a subdivision of the shire or County. But this leaves unanswered the question, what is it a hundred of? The answer seems to be that it was a hundred 'hide'. Then the question arises, what was a hide? Nothing to do with animal skins, the word in this sense was used to indicate an area of land that could be tilled by one plough. Since that area would not be the same in all parts of the country (ploughing being more difficult in hilly areas) no uniform or precise measures can be given. But very roughly, a hide was around one hundred acres. So the Lowland Hundred could be of the order of 10,000 acres.

About 3,500 B.C. a major rise in the level of the sea resulted in coastal submergence, followed by a massive inundation. There is abundant geological evidence in this area for the truth of

The submerged forest in Cardigan Bay: Tree stumps around the Dyfi estuary

this account of events: the remains of the tree stumps of the submerged forests can be seen around the Dyfi estuary at low tide.

The Lord of Ceridigion at that time was Gwyddno Garanhir. He was very wealthy, owning much land, none of which was as fruitful as the part called 'Cantre'r Gwaelod'. The area supported a large population and the Lowland Hundred was so low-lying that it had to be protected from the encroachment of the sea by strong walls or dykes which had to be kept in constant repair. Lord Gwyddno Garanhir entrusted this responsibility to Prince Seithennin, one of his warriors. Guards were posted at intervals along the walls to watch for weaknesses in the structure. Seithennin, however, was a drunkard who spent much of his time in feasting and drinking, and so neglected his duty.

One night a storm arose and the strong South-Westerlies blew the raging waves against the weakening walls of the 'Cantre'r Gwaelod'. Finally, the walls were breached and the whole area inundated.

Manua, the largest city of the Hundred, with its wide streets and costly buildings, is now a silent city. Yet not always silent, for now and then distant chimes sound low and sweet above the lullaby of the sea in the long summer evenings, or sometimes by night, rising mysteriously from the depths of the sea.

The remains of the old boundaries of the 'Cantre'r Gwaelod' are still there. Sarn y Bwch, a submerged reef of huge stones, extends for about two miles into the sea from just north of the mouth of the River Dysynni, while between Borth and Aberystwyth, Sarn Cynfelin marks the southern boundary, stretching out for nearly eight miles. Starting as a narrow strip, the western end expands into a pear shape with boulders considerably larger than the ones nearer the shore.

This area is known to seafaring folk as 'the patches'. Both these reefs are a danger to shipping, so their extremities are marked by buoys which are maintained by Trinity House.

ABERDYFI CASTLE

In approximately 1150, Rhys, the son of Gruffydd, Prince of South Wales, crossed the River Dyfi from Ceredigion (Dyfed), accompanied by the Bishop of St David's. Rhys must have been impressed with the strategic position of the hill in the centre of Aberdyfi, for in 1151 he built a castle on the site, which is mentioned in Brut-y-Tywysogion ('The Record of the Princes').

It was possibly a typical 'motte and bailey' castle or more probably a castle of wattle and daub which was defended by a stockade. Many of the castles built by the Welsh and the early Norman invaders are believed to be of this kind. Sited on almost impregnable rock, the castle needed little fortification.

It appears that Aberdyfi Castle was destroyed about the year 1157 by the Earl Robert de Clare, one of the Norman Lords in Wales. There is no trace of the structure today.

On a chart of the Dyfi estuary prepared by Lewis Morris, a customs officer in Aberdyfi in 1748, the rocky hill was named Bryn Celwydd ('The Hill of Lies'). The origin of this name is uncertain but it may have arisen from the gossip exchanged by local women as they collected on the hill to wave goodbye to their husbands embarking on a long voyage.

By the year 1845, the hill was known to local residents as Pen-y-Bryn ('Head of the Hill') and in 1897, a local landowner made a gift of a shelter to be erected on its highest point. The original cost of the structure was £30. It has become a favourite vantage point for both residents and visitors to the village. Pen-y-Bryn has looked down silently on many changes in the village and on the river.

Today, however, with the growing corruption of Welsh place names, Pen-y-Bryn has been superseded by the inappropriate name 'The Bandstand'. Despite this it remains a site of historical interest and one of the unchanging focal points in a changing landscape.

Pen-y-Bryn dominates the centre of the village

THE BEAR OF AMSTERDAM

Aberdyfi briefly entered the international scene in the days of Good Queen Bess, when the greatest adventure of the Elizabethan age disturbed the peaceful waters of the River Dyfi.

When Drake's Navy scattered the Spanish Armada, one of the surviving galleons staggered around Scotland, across the Irish Sea and found its way into the Dyfi estuary. She was the 'Bear of Amsterdam', a caravel of 120 tons, with a crew of sixty-five Spaniards. She anchored in mid-river, causing much excitement along the banks of the Dyfi.

The militia of Merionethshire and Cardiganshire assembled and waited for an opportunity to take or destroy the ship, but as there were no boats available she could not be boarded, and unfortunately there were no cannons to hole her. So there she swung at anchor with the military forces of two counties standing helplessly by, unable to do more than fire the odd musket-shot.

The Bear of Amsterdam

The 1953 Bear of Amsterdam

Someone had the idea of building fire-rafts up-river which would float down and set fire to the galleon, but this proved to be ineffective. The prevailing winds on this coast are westerlies, and blow from the open sea into the estuary, so that it was difficult for the 'Bear of Amsterdam' to sail out. However, after several days of watching and waiting, the wind changed and the Spanish ship was able to sail away into the open sea, where one of Drake's ships was waiting to capture her.

During the celebrations for the coronation of the second Queen Elizabeth in 1953, Aberdyfi people took the opportunity to complete an unfinished task. A boat was rigged up to represent the 'Bear of Amsterdam' and anchored in mid-river. Watched by hundreds of onlookers it was set on fire to provide a fitting start to the new Elizabethan era.

It is said that, at night, unseen by anyone, some members of the crew swam ashore and hid in the surrounding hills. They were never caught and eventually merged with local people. A Spanish strain of dark brown skin with dark hair may have come to the area from this source.

THE STORY OF THE ABERDYFI LIFEBOATS

Though Aberdyfi is remote from the industrial centres of Britain, during the nineteenth century the effects of the Industrial Revolution were felt even here. The once quiet shore was alive with the sights, sounds and smells of a busy harbour.

Virtually everyone in the village was involved with the sea in one way or another. The port grew rapidly, with ships coming and going on every tide to all parts of the world. In the ship-building yards located on the banks of the River Dyfi boats of all shapes and sizes were produced. Many of these were subsequently lost, some in foreign waters. Others met their fate in local coastal areas.

In 1837 the first lifeboat arrived at Aberdyfi. She was a rowing and sailing non-self-righting boat called 'Victoria'. This boat was housed in a stone building especially built on the beach in Penhelig. The west side gable-end had a wide doorway through which the boat was taken out on its wheeled carriage along the village street to one of a number of convenient places giving easy access to the river. Today this building is used as a dwelling house, and is known as 'Traeth Dyfi'. The row of cottages opposite this building was known as 'Lifeboat Terrace'.

In 1858, the 'Victoria' was replaced by another boat, which was never formally named. Costing £146 to build, her launching carriage cost the community an extra £47. She was a six-oared self-righting type of vessel and she stayed in Aberdyfi for seven years.

In 1865 she was replaced by a ten-oared self-righting boat called the 'Royal Berkshire'. To build her cost £252 and her launching carriage was put at £86. This boat remained at the station for twenty-one years and was often called out for rescue work.

The first boathouse in Penhelig

The new lifeboat house in Penhelig, 1903. Crew (L to R) Thomas Jones (Coxwain), D. Davies, Police Constable Jones, Siencyn Owen, John Simon Richards, John Rees (Stevedor), David Jones (Mervinia), John Lloyd, Richard Davies (Customs), Lewis Hughes, Evan Roberts, Owen Owen, Owen Williams, Charles Thomas

In 1886 a larger size of lifeboat appeared in the village. She was the 'Thomas Nicolls Stratford', an improved type of vessel which had cost £359 to build. A new launching carriage, costing £120, was also provided.

It was now thought necessary to find a new and more convenient building to accommodate the lifeboat. A site in Penhelig was purchased for £150 and a new boathouse built at a cost of £400.

Coxswain Tom Jones supervising a launching

Though housed in this brand new building, the lifeboat still had to be pulled along the main road for launching into the river. This was felt to be very inconvenient and time-consuming, so a new slipway was constructed opposite the new boathouse in 1903 at a cost of £309. This slipway can still be seen today, though now much worn by the passing years and the action of the waves.

A new 35-foot double-banked, self-righting boat now arrived in Aberdyfi. She had ten oars, masts and sail, and a sliding or drop keel. She was built at a cost of £865 and was named the

A lifeboat lowered down the slipway in 1903

'William Brocksop' at a ceremony in September 1904. She was launched with no difficulty into the river by means of the new slipway, and on her return the heavy boat was hauled up the slipway by ropes connected to an eight-armed capstan.

These were exciting occasions for us village children. We watched fascinated as the capstan clicked round and the men chanted and sang. The work required a large gang of men summoned from all parts of the village by the firing of a rocket. Normally there were four practice launches a year in addition to the more serious calls.

Occasionally there was a night launching, which were truly memorable occasions. Dozens of oil lamps glowed in the darkness as orders

Eight-armed capstan hauling the lifeboat up the slipway

Lifeboat Day, August Bank Holiday Monday, 1921

were shouted in stentorian voices. These were men who were used to working at sea in gale-force winds; some of them had good reason to be grateful to the Lifeboat Institution when they themselves had been in danger.

August Bank Holiday Monday was always Lifeboat Day, when the lifeboat was drawn along the village street on its wheeled carriage by two strong farm horses(with the assistance of the local children!)

The new type of rescue craft, 1963

When the shipping and ship-building industries declined during the early years of the 20th century, there was little other commercial activity in the area to take its place. Soon the pier was deserted and the wharf became the site of a coal dump. The men who once sailed to all parts of the world were now ashore, with time on their hands. To earn a livelihood many of them turned to salmon-fishing in the upper reaches of the River Dyfi, and hiring out boats to holiday visitors. During the winter months they tried their hand at gathering mussels from the bed of the river. Many tons of these mussels were sent to the busy Midland market.

The 'William Brocksop' was withdrawn from service in 1921, and her place was taken by the 'George and Margaret'. But ultimately, because of the decline in shipping, there was no further need for a lifeboat in Aberdyfi. And so in 1931 the station was closed and the boathouse was sold. It has since been converted into a dwelling house.

But the story of the Aberdyfi lifeboats does not end there. Recently, with the increasing popularity of all forms of water sports and other activities, safety at sea has become an important consideration. In 1963 the R.N.L.I. introduced a new type of rescue craft to deal with situations where speedboats are involved. A station was subsequently established at the Outward Bound School. In 1991 a larger boat was inaugurated, with a launching tractor. Then the R.N.L.I and the Dovey Yacht Club built new premises on the shore next to the pier. This houses the new lifeboat, now manned by trained personnel.

THE STANDING STONE IN TYWYN (Y GROESFAEN)

It is said that there are over 10,000 standing stones and other ancient memorials in Britain. One of the least known stands close to the main road between Tywyn and Bryncrug, about two hundred yards east of the Tywyn cemetery.

It has always surprised me that Y Groesfaen near Tywyn has been neglected, and not preserved as an ancient monument and an attraction for tourists. This tall pillar is described in the Merioneth Volume of the Royal Commission on Ancient Monuments in Wales as:

'A fine boulder of volcanic origin, 7ft 6ins high ... broken at the top and the Cross may have been inscribed upon this ....'

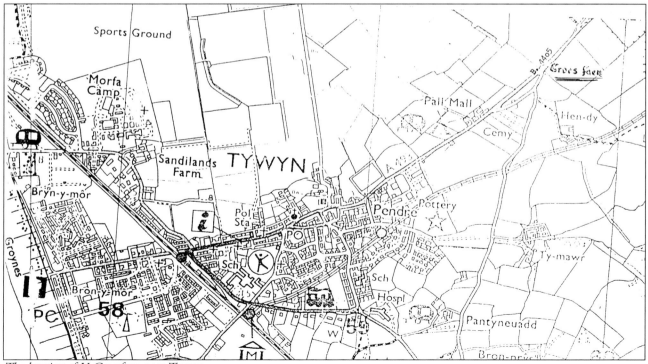

The location of Y Groesfaen near Tywyn

Y Groesfaen

Standing Stones were erected throughout the Principality as the tide of Christian religion flowed slowly across the land. Missionary monks who brought religion to Wales would hold their meetings at the site of such crosses, and before it was possible to erect a building, the Gospel was taught around a cross.

This particular shaft was moved in 1840 to Morfa Cadvan, but was later returned to the original site. This is probably the reason why there is no pedestal, the pillar being sunk directly into the ground.

Before this interesting and holy relic disappears completely, it should be cleaned, pulled upright and railed round.

THE TYWYN PIER (1876–77)

Towyn, or Tywyn, is a small town situated on the mouth of the river from which it derives its appellation. It is much frequented in the bathing season, the shore being delightful for either riding or bathing, and some good specimens of conchology are to be met with on the beach. The inhabitants are chiefly employed in the herring fisheries; and a small coasting trade is carried on. A valuable slate quarry has lately been opened, and there are also several lead and copper mines in the vicinity. The church is a small neat structure. Here are chapels for dissenters; and a free-school and some alms-houses, endowed by charitable individuals. St. Cadvan's well here is held in estimation for its medicinal properties; and the streams in the neighbourhood afford good sport to the angler. In many respects Towyn presents many attractions to the visitor; the surrounding country is beautiful, and embellished with many seats of the gentry of the county.

from 'Dugdale's 'Guide to Tywyn' (1835-45)

Many people must have wondered why the road from Tywyn railway station to the sea is called 'Pier Road' when there is no pier to be seen. In fact the name is all that is left to record an imaginative but disastrous mid-Victorian enterprise.

British enthusiasm for the seaside was widespread in the 19th century and sea-bathing became all the rage. In 1876 it was decided to construct a pier and landing-place for passengers on the Tywyn seafront. A company was formed, called the Tywyn Pier Company Ltd, to raise a capital of £12,000 with shares at £5 each. The promoters were William Parry Esq. (Tywyn), R.G. Price (wine merchant, Tywyn), O. Daniel (auctioneer, Tywyn), Richard Hammond (cabinet-maker, Tywyn), Robert Jones Roberts (druggist, Tywyn), J. Hughes Jones (merchant, Aberdyfi) and Edwin Jones (schoolmaster, The Academy, Tywyn).

The opening ceremony presented a remarkable spectacle. When the site of the new pier had been marked out and a line of white stakes driven into the sands, people flocked to the seashore. They formed themselves into a procession, headed by the Aberdyfi band. The town crier went out and about while the bells in St Cadfan's Church were rung. That evening the whole scene was lit up with a fireworks display.

The foundation stone for the pier was laid in 1877 and work continued apace. However, when the pier was only half-built a ferocious storm washed it away. Work was suspended and not long after the company was wound up (11th November 1879).

Was the Tywyn Pier project a visionary scheme for the future of the town or a badly thought-out business gamble? Perhaps like most schemes of this kind, a bit of both. The sentiments expressed in the folowing poem by J.E. Roberts, alas, never came to fruition.

Fine terraces shall tower
Along the beach one day;
A well constructed Pier
Shall meet old Neptune's fray;
Canoes and craft for hire
Shall fleetly cross our sea;
And boats that swarm with tourists
Shall traverse to our quay

No more shall Aberystwyth
Nor Barmouth proud excel;
'Tis on the charms of Towyn
The visitors shall dwell!
A safe and glorious shore.
As queen of watering places
Stands Towyn evermore!

ABERDYFI'S MYTHICAL BEAST

On the gable-end of a house high above the centre of Aberdyfi, not far from the Parish Church, stands a little-noticed feature about which there is scant information.

From a distance it appears to be some kind of mythical or heraldic bird (the house was once known as 'Eagle House'), but on closer inspection it looks more like a griffin or even a dragon. The bird or beast is made of terracotta and clings to the ridge of the roof with its front claws and powerful tail. Its short wings are furled and it carries some kind of ball in its beak.

The house used to have close connections with the sea. 'Eagle House' was previously known as 'Customs House' and was occupied by Lewis Morris, the eldest of four notable Morris brothers who hailed from Anglesey. He was a poet, scholar, musician, botanist, mining engineer, expert navigator and marine surveyor.

In 1748 he was entrusted with the task of making a survey of the Welsh ports, and between 1751 and 1756 he acted as Customs Officer at Aberdyfi.

House at Aberdyfi, showing the mythical beast

Later the house was occupied by a well-known seafaring family which could boast no fewer than six sea captains among its sons.

Could it be that one of these captains, on giving up his command and retiring to Aberdyfi, had the stone creature set up in a commanding

Aberdyfi's mythical beast

position above the river? Maybe it was done in imitation of the famous Liver Bird, which surveys the River Mersey from the top of the twin towers of the Liver Building in Liverpool. It is interesting to note that the Liver Bird carries a piece of seaweed in its beak whilst the Aberdyfi creature is carrying a round object in its mouth.

It is possible that the object or ball is meant to represent the world: a fitting symbol of the mariner's connection with global travel and trade. The mystery remains.

A DEEP REMINDER OF THE PAST

The sweeping effects of the Industrial Revolution, an increasing population with the consequent boom in building needs, together with the demands of the Navy for copper to sheathe the bottom of their ships, led to much mining work in the mountains behind Aberdyfi when seams of copper and lead were found at the beginning of the 18th century.

It is possible that the lead mines of Bryndinas, Tyddyn-y-Briddell and Melin Llyn Pair in Cwm Maethlon (popularly known as 'Happy Valley') were first worked by the Romans.

Production from these mines was irregular and ceased around 1880. Only a few remains can be seen today.

It is highly likely that Copper Hill Street derived its name from this activity and that miners lived there.

The cave above Nantiesyn

The author by the cave above Nantiesyn

Following recent excavation works, carried out above Nantiesyn, a cave has been discovered. It is a dark, damp place penetrating into the heart of the mountain, which is honeycombed by passages called 'levels' going in many directions and interspersed with some deep shafts. The cave serves as a sad reminder of this once busy industry.

There are several other caves in this area. One has its entrance behind Glandovey Terrace and is connected with the Balkan Hill workings. Some of these caves were strategically placed near the quayside, making easier loading into the ships which carried away the products obtained by the hard-working miners.

CWM MAETHLON (HAPPY VALLEY)

When the Turnpike Trust was established in 1775, a road was built to connect Machynlleth with Tywyn. In those days, Aberdyfi was considered to be of such little importance that it was completely ignored and the road went through a quiet unspoilt valley called Cwm Maethlon, which is today known as Happy Valley. It was obviously thought of as a valley of contentment.

At a hamlet called Cwrt, near Pennal, this turnpike road branches off the A493 and approaches a formidable range of high mountains, dominated by Tarren Cwm Ffernol (1768 ft). The valley is narrow and has a wild beauty. After about half a mile one reaches another adjacent valley called Cwm Ffernol (the Infernal Valley) which is a deep gorge, having a fast flowing stream called Nant Cwmffernol.

The old coach road now rises steeply by twists and turns until one reaches the highest point at Pant-y-Carneddau, a wild, desolate place littered with volcanic rocks. From here the road starts its gradual descent through the valley, overlooked on the north side by Corlan Fraith (1332 ft), while the southern side of the valley

The mysterious lake known as 'Bearded Lake', connected with legend

Maethlon Chapel

is marked by a range of mountains called Cefn-Rhos-Uchaf. Here, Mynydd-y-Llyn overlooks Llyn Barfog (Bearded Lake), whose dark waters contain no fish. It is surrounded by wild rugged hills where the deep silence is broken only by the sad call of the curlew.

Legend tells us that this area is a favourite haunt of Plant Annwn (the children of Elfin Land). It is said that a very large hairy monster lived in the lake, and that the name 'bearded' derives from this creature. It was dragged out of the lake by King Arthur's horse, and in doing so a mark was left on a rock nearby which can still be seen today. It is called Carn March Arthur (King Arthur's Horse Hoof).

When copper and lead were found in these mountains, mines were opened at Tyddyn-y-Briddell where the remains can be seen today, showing that much activity took place here from 1752.

The valley now widens and is much less austere, so that the road winds among softly rounded mountains, beautifully green with vegetation. There are several farmsteads to be seen with sheep and cattle grazing the lush fields. Sometimes one can see dogs collecting sheep from distant fields, controlled by a shepherd standing on the old coach road.

A brook, Afon Dyffryn Gwyn, now runs parallel with the road which soon reaches a small chapel standing in a lovely quiet part of the valley. This building was erected in 1885 to serve the several farms in the valley, who in those days had large staffs of domestics and farm workers.

A graveyard is attached to the chapel and it is surprising to find that many Aberdyfi people have been buried here, especially as the journey from Aberdyfi involved a long climb up the mountain behind the village and a steep descent on the valley side. A two-horse bier was used to carry the coffins along the mountain tracks and paths.

A prominent monument stands in this little graveyard. It was erected by the inhabitants of Aberdyfi in memory of one William Radcliffe, the village schoolmaster who was drowned in the River Dyfi in 1867 at the age of twenty-three years. A very well known Aberdyfi doctor was also buried in this peaceful spot in 1873. Dr John Pughe was the leader of a religious sect called the Plymouth Brethren. He held several important positions in Aberdyfi and indeed in the whole area.

Continuing along the road through the valley, more evidence of extensive mining activity is found in an area known as Melin-Llyn-Pair, where lead ore was produced, off and on, between 1741 and 1882, after which date the industry faded out. Before the coming of the National Grid, this area was chosen to provide the district with electricity by utilising water-power from the little brook. It proved insufficient however to meet the demand, so oil-engine plants were installed to augment the water power.

Still continuing in a westerly direction for a few more miles, the old turnpike road now rejoins the main A493 road from Tywyn to Aberdyfi. This second turnpike road was made in 1828 to supersede the Happy Valley road, which has now reclaimed its privacy and quietness so that it can indeed be called a 'Valley of Contentment'.

The entrance to Happy Valley

THE MARINERS' BEACON

During the nineteenth century, the port of Aberdyfi grew rapidly, with ships coming and going on every tide. From this small fishing village in an obscure part of the world were despatched slates and slabs from the quarries of Corris, Aberllefni and Abergynolwyn. Timber was imported from Newfoundland, wheat from the Mediterranean and phosphates and nitrates from South America. Coal, potatoes and cattle were landed here, while limestone was imported in large quantities.

As a result of all this activity in Cardigan Bay, Aberdyfi was granted official recognition as a Trinity Port. Subsequently, the first Admiralty Chart of the wide and treacherous Aberdyfi Estuary was published in 1835, and the channel was marked with buoys.

With so many foreign ships entering Cardigan Bay, an additional navigational aid was constructed in 1880 on Pen-y-Bwch, a prominent hill to the north of Aberdyfi. Here the Trinity House Brethren erected a 40-foot high timber construction at a cost of £70. Painted white, it allowed a ship's captain to take a bearing from 30 miles out at sea. As a result this 'Mariners' Beacon' became an important

The Mariner's Beacon, 1880

landmark in the area, aiding safe navigation in the busy waters of the bay.

The official name given to the beacon was 'Bwch Head'. No doubt the name was derived from the name of one of the old boundaries of the legendary 'Cantre'r Gwaelod' (Lowland Hundred), the area of land that was submerged by the sea in the sixth century. 'Sarn Bwch' is a submerged reef of large stones stretching out about two miles into the sea from a point just north of the River Dysynni. Many ships have been wrecked on this reef. Local people know the hill as 'Y Polyn Gwyn' but in time the name became anglicised to 'Beacon Hill'.

The beginning of the century witnessed the decline of shipping activity in Cardigan Bay. The Mariners' Beacon began to lose its importance. Then came the Second World War, when the waters of Cardigan Bay were disturbed by shells fired from heavy AA guns at Tonfanau army camp at the foot of Beacon Hill. Although the beacon was regularly maintained by Trinity House, its exposed position caused gradual deterioration of its timber structure and before long this well-known landmark disappeared from the local scene.

It is still a pleasure to visit Beacon Hill however. From the summit there is a view of great beauty. Some six hundred feet below stretch the constantly moving waters of Cardigan Bay. On a clear day one can see the island of Bardsey and the Lleyn peninsula to the north, while to the south the Pembrokeshire coastline can be picked out. Inland there are wonderful views of the Dysynni Valley, as well as three of the highest mountains in Wales, Snowdon, Cader Idris, and Plynlimon.

THE VILLAGE BLACKSMITH

In the early twenties the blacksmith's (or smithy as it was more popularly known) was a busy and important place. Here I was allowed free access, indeed, I wondered in and out of t he smithy whenever I liked. The roar of the blacksmith's bellows reached my ears before I got anywhere near the building. I found him pumping away at the bellows to fan the coals to glowing red. I watched him draw the white hot iron from the fire amidst a shower of sparks and beat it into shape on the anvil.

The village smithy

Sometimes I arrived to find him with a horse's hoof in his leathered lap, filing it with long steady strokes.

In fact, the whole shoeing process was a constant source of surprise to me. The smith stood with his back to the horse's leg, lifted its foot by a tuft of hair and anchored it between his knees, his leather apron being split up the middle to allow for this. The smith then pared and hammered, in what appeared to me to be a most abandoned way, without the slightest protest from the horse.

But by far the most awe-inspiring part of the process for me was the moment when the red-hot shoe, held in long tongs, was pressed to the hoof, the acrid smoke spurting out from the sides, producing a smell I always liked. When the smith was satisfied that the shoe was an exact match for the hoof he would plunge the shoe into a small water tank beneath the forge to cool it before nailing it to the hoof, dextrously cutting off the points of the nails which came through the sloping sides.

Beside shoeing, the other spectacular process at the smithy was the hooping of cartwheels and this was done on the road outside. The wheel was clamped onto a circular metal plate while a band previously made to fit was heating in the fire. The blacksmith pumped away at the bellows, from time to time moving the band to ensure that it was evenly heated. When it was ready several men grabbed it with tongs and rushed it out to the waiting wheel. There was a strong smell of burning wood as the hot band was hammered home. Water from buckets standing in readiness was thrown, hissing and steaming, over the wheel to contract the band and ensure a tight fit.

What a useful place the smithy's was when the early motor cars appeared on the scene! The smith was kept very busy carrying out repairs on parts which continually needed attention.

The blacksmith's was a place of intense work but also it was a place for opinions to be shared. The old men of the village used to meet there and the subject most often under discussion was religion. The sermon of the previous Sunday was dissected and perhaps pulled to pieces. On the other hand there was much praise. Our blacksmith was very well read and he became the impromptu chairman of the meeting.

ABERDYFI CEMETERY

Though countless people are immortalised in churchyards and cemeteries up and down the land, they are only remembered for a short time by their friends and relations, and rarely does the gravestone earn them a passing thought from anyone who did not know them during their lives.

It is only by a person's deeds that he or she is remembered. We must be content to make our mark, however insignificant, on humanity during our lives, and cannot expect to be thanked after we are dead.

On a recent sunny summer's day I paid a visit to the cemetery on the main road between Aberdyfi and Tywyn, and wandered among the headstones where hundreds of people of the area have been laid to rest during the last century. There was an atmosphere of peace and tranquillity there, and I had time to reflect on times past.

Here were inscribed the names, occupations and dates of birth and death of the persons buried beneath. Here were the family connections and, invariably, a short verse or religious text. The history of my village thus lay displayed before me, and as I read the names I

Aberdyfi Cemetery

was transported to the days of my childhood over 80 years ago.

There were people here whom I had much respected, indeed admired, people who had faced up bravely to the vicissitudes and hardships of those days. I knew most of these good people whose gravestones reflected the social hierarchy and social divisions of those days. But even in death people were segregated between church and chapel.

Aberdyfi lies within the parish of Tywyn, the mother church of which is the ancient and well-known church of St Cadfan. It was in the churchyard of St Cadfan's that the early inhabitants of Aberdyfi were buried. As there was no road between Aberdyfi and Tywyn in those days, the funeral cortege had to travel along the shore over soft sand and through a marsh. It was a heavy task involving relays of men known as 'bearers', who took turns to carry the load.

The village hearse outside Aberdyfi Cemetary, late 1800

Other burials took place in a graveyard adjoining the little chapel in Happy Valley, known as Maethlon. Here again a long journey was involved: the mourners had to climb the mountain behind the village and then descend the steep slope on the other side. A horse-bier was used to carry the coffins along mountain tracks. In the ancient church of Llangelynnin on the edge of the sea between Tywyn and Llwyngwril there can be seen a two-horse bier hanging on the wall near the north entrance. This is believed to be the only one now in existence.

As the population of Aberdyfi grew between 1840 and 1880, the parish churchyard in Tywyn could no longer serve the needs of the village. And so in 1885 a new cemetery was established on the hillside facing the sea to the west of Aberdyfi.

As I continued walking round the graves, I could not help noticing that a maritime connection is prominent. Here lie ship captains, master mariners and chief officers, whilst ordinary seamen are legion. Shore-based occupations are represented by ship-builders, carpenters, and chandlers, as well as sail-makers, blacksmiths and fishermen. The Aberdyfi mariners who travelled to all parts of the world, found it was very necessary to learn foreign languages and indeed out of politeness many

spoke fluent Spanish. I well remember how these seafaring men used to congregate around a seat on the Aberdyfi waterfront, known as Llawr Gang or 'Boatmens' Seat.' There they would chat, often in Spanish, and recall the glories of days gone by. Boys were not allowed amongst that select gathering, but sometimes I managed to intrude quietly into their midst and heard many fantastic tales of distant wanderings and exotic places. Any boy caught listening received prompt punishment in the form of a kick from the boot of a stern disciplinarian, but I felt the risk was well worth taking for the incredible stories I heard.

Most of the gravestones in the cemetery have an obvious Welsh connection, with names like Evans, Owen, Pugh, Jones and Thomas prominent. But there are some which, in complete contrast, carry an English inscription. Quite often these seem to belong to tradesmen, such as carters, farriers, grooms and coachmen, who, before the coming of the motor-car, were active in the neighbourhood. All have now disappeared, as have the railway fraternity.

The people of the village faithfully attended every funeral, where there was an accepted etiquette to be observed. Funerals in those days were most impressive occasions. In the house of mourning the window blinds were drawn and until the day of the funeral village folk, young and old, would visit the house to pay their last respects. On the day of the funeral a private service in the house was followed by a slow procession to a church or chapel where a fairly long service was held. The vicar or minister usually knew the deceased personally and in his address he recounted all the good the person had done in the past and how much he or she would be missed in the future. There were other orations and, of course, the magnificent rendering of hymns with wonderful harmony.

The service over, the cortege would form up outside and proceed to the cemetery. All the houses it passed would have their blinds drawn. All traffic would stop to allow the dead to take

A two-horse bier

Garden of Rest, Aberdyfi Cemetery, 1980

precedence. Led by the clergy and ministers, the procession was marshalled by some self-appointed men who controlled it all with much authority. Next the men of the village had to walk in pairs for the two-mile journey to the cemetery. Then came the horse-drawn hearse driven by a local farmer. He supplied the horse as he was the milkman who delivered milk to the household. Behind the hearse came the male relatives of the deceased. The family women mourners were conveyed in cabs, which later on were superseded by motor cars. Other women wishing to attend the funeral would join the rear of the procession.

At the final committal ceremony there would be beautiful singing appropriate to the occasion, which had a therapeutic effect on the assembled gathering. In those days it was respectful to wear mourning and men wore black armbands and women as much black as they could afford. Once back in the village everyone was expected to go to the bereaved house for tea. With so many folk in the house, all talking about various subjects, the tea party went some way to help the bereaved forget their loss.

A very early Welsh custom was to make a village contribution towards the funeral expenses. It was made known that the front room of a certain house would be available. Here a rota of two people would sit with a bowl covered by a plate. On entering you would place a coin on the plate. This was recorded and the plate was tipped so that the coin joined others in the bowl. When the bowl containing the money was handed over to the bereaved family together with the names and the amounts of the contributions, this list was carefully kept and referred to when other funerals took place in the village. It was a case of communal help. Today the Social Services have done away with this very admirable spirit of neighbourliness.

By the year 1953 the village cemetery was getting short of space, so part of the mountainside graveyard was fenced off and set aside to provide additional accommodation.

The old cemetery had many elaborate gravestones, some having a nautical theme, with ships' anchors, etc. The council now brought in new regulations: no gravestone was to exceed one metre in height and the use of kerb stones was forbidden. The contrast between the two sections of the graveyard is now apparent and shows how necessary it was to make these regulations.

With cremation becoming an accepted alternative to burial, an area at the top of the cemetery was set aside for the interment of cremated ashes. In 1980 a Garden of Rest was established here, with flower beds and the surrounding walls topped with slate slabs for memorial tablets. This was the first Garden of Rest to be made in the County of Merioneth.

Thus it is that changes that have taken place in the village in the last hundred years are reflected in the changing face of the Aberdyfi Cemetery.

EARLY FARMING ACTIVITY

By Oliver Gabriel

My English friends in Rhoslefain are very anxious to know how our ancestors lived and worked in the area from the late 1880s to the 1920s. Being the descendent of a family that has resided in Rhoslefain since 1850, I have learned the history of the district through listening to my parents and their contemporaries.

Rhoslefain was a farming area with several smallholdings and sizeable farms, a Post Office and general stores, a school, church, two chapels and a smithy. All the smallholdings in the area were three to ten acres and they all kept one or two cows, which provided them with milk and butter. Chickens produced eggs and an occasional roast chicken for dinner, or an old hen, called a broiler, which made lovely chicken broth.

Also, a couple of pigs would be kept, which provided bacon throughout the year. Fresh meat was very seldom eaten. Bacon fried or boiled was always the mid-day meal, with plenty of potatoes, carrots and swedes and a glass of butter-milk. In order to have sufficient potatoes for the whole year, an agreement was made with a neighbouring farmer to plant a few rows of potatoes in his field, in return for which we would help with his shearing or with the hay harvest.

Whilst I am on the subject of food and making your mouths water, I must not forget bread, the staff of life.

Every cottage and farmhouse had a built-in bread oven. The oven was heated by burning wood until the brick lining was white with heat. Then the charcoal was raked out, leaving a thin layer. Tins were filled with dough and placed in the oven. The door was shut tightly for a couple of hours, and when it was opened the lovely smell of fresh bread would fill the room.

There was no running water in any house until after the First World War. Water had to be carried to the house from the stream or well. This made a woman's life very hard, as a lot of water is used by a family during the day. There were rainwater butts beside every house to catch as much water as possible.

The only sanitary arrangement was an earth closet at the end of the garden.

Candles and paraffin lamps were the only method of lighting the house.

Early farming activity on the hills of Aberdyfi overlooking the Dyfi estuary

The men living in the smallholdings were employed on the bigger farms, others on the railway, looking after the tracks from the Dysynni to Llangelynin. Others were employed at Tonfanau Granite Quarry. Most of the products of this quarry were used in the local building trade. There were several skilled men working there making lintels for doors and windows. They would break and trim the stones to the architect's measurements. All this work was done with hammers and chisels, and its results are to be seen in all the towns and villages in the area.

The wives of these men found another source of income after their children went to school. A dozen of them used to go down to the beach between Tonfanau and Felin Fraenan to gather seaweed. This was a special kind of seaweed much in demand in South Wales for making laver bread. Winkles were also plentiful on the beach at Felin Fraenan. All this could only be done when the tide was favourable, as the seaweed had to be carried to Tonfanau station. It was then sent by rail to Swansea.

I understand that people were friendly in those days, always ready to help in some way when there was illness or death. Walking was the only way to get to work, and the working day was very long, from dawn to dusk.

People were very religious in those days. This was the time of the religious revival, when no work was done on Sundays and everyone attended the services. Nobody thought of harvesting the hay on a Sunday, even though the weather might be favourable.

It was a generation of men and women that worked extremely hard under very difficult conditions and received very little monetary reward for it.

We must be thankful that much progress has been made since those days, which has made our lives much easier.

FAR FROM HOME

The 13th century church that serves the area around the village of Llanegryn in Meirionnydd is situated high above the village in the basin of the River Dysynni. It is a simple, beautiful church in the Perpendicular style, surrounded by a churchyard where hundreds of Llanegryn people have been laid to rest.

To walk among the tombstones and headstones that record the names and occupations of the people of this area during the last three centuries gives one a feeling of peace and tranquillity.

The church at Llanegryn

On a recent visit, as I strolled along the path towards the church porch, my attention was drawn to a strange name on a long marble tombstone, Dr F.H.V. Grosholz. The name was rather different to the more familiar surnames on other headstones such as Evans, Owen, Pugh, Jones, Thomas, Rees and Richards. The tombstone, with an English inscription, was of further interest:

TO THE MEMORY OF
DR. F.H.V. GROSHOLZ
who for upwards of 20 years practised
as a Physician at Towyn and Aberdovey
and was greatly beloved for his untiring
devotion to all in need or sickness.
He died June 21st 1898 aged 45 years.
This stone was erected by a few friends
as a small token of their great regard.

It was then I remembered that, during my childhood, the name of Dr Grosholz had often been mentioned by older people and always with much respect.

With some further research, I was able to discover more about this remarkable man who had lived over one hundred years ago.

When the first of many regattas was held in Aberdovey, on the 30th August, 1880, Dr Grosholz was the Hon. Secretary of the organising committee.

In a Trade Directory dated 1891, covering the Tywyn and Aberdyfi area, Dr Grosholz was described as being born in Baden-Baden in Germany and a 'Surgeon and Physician living in Gothic House, Towyn' and by 1895 he was Medical Officer of Health for Towyn Urban District Council.

In view of these very close connections with Tywyn and Aberdyfi one is left to wonder why Dr Frederick Hamer V. Grosholz was buried in this quiet country churchyard and, indeed, how someone with a possible German or Austrian background, came to spend his final years in the area, particularly in the latter days of the Victorian Age. Thus a number of questions remain unanswered.

Dr F.H.V. Grosholz's tombstone in Llanegryn churchyard

EARLY HOME LIFE

One of my first memories of Aberdyfi is of a silence that was broken only by the cry of the seagulls as I looked through our front room window at the Dyfi River. There was a feeling of tranquillity and security which is as strong now as it was then and for which I shall always be thankful.

I was born in 1910, not many years before the world was to be embroiled in the First World War. One of my first memories is of a local man dressed as a soldier, carrying a rifle and weighed down with canvas packs, walking past our house towards the railway station. He was going back to war following a short period of leave. Little did I think that one day, some thirty years later, I would also be re-enacting the same experience in another war, leaving this timeless haven of calm for a turbulent way of life with so much destruction.

I am thankful that this secluded spot was spared to be a wonderful place in which to live. The children of the village, as in many similar Welsh places, were fortunate to be born into this comparatively unsophisticated way of life but which still had many natural riches to offer.

Children playing in one of the natural pools left behind by the receding tide, about 1900

I can clearly remember that the very young boys wore sailor suits but these were soon changed for jerseys and shorts which were more comfortable and durable. Boots, not shoes, were the standard footwear, with light sandals during the summer. Often, of course, we went bare-footed. During cold, wet weather in winter there were leather leggings to be worn which were long and buttoned up. Most boys hated wearing them as they seemed to restrict our freedom and our play.

Mothers became very resourceful in patching and cutting garments to size. The most adventurous would create suits for their sons and skirts for their daughters, but the man who really counted in these matters was the local tailor, a splendid character who visited the house to carry out his expert alterations. I never had a proper suit as a young boy, but had to be content with short trousers, a grey jersey and long grey stockings with coloured rings around the tops. No boy got long trousers until he reached fourteen or fifteen years old and then he was so self-conscious that he had to be pushed out of the house to go to church or other places of importance, wishing with every step that the ground would open up and swallow him. Alongside the skills of mothers with clothing alterations were the undoubted abilities of fathers to repair boots and shoes for their families, thus saving considerable money for the other needs of the home.

A boy might come to school on a Monday in the coat and trousers his brother had been wearing the previous Friday. In the cruel way of children those who wore these clothes were often the butt of teasing even though the teasers were in the same situation.

There were clothing clubs in those days and salesmen would call each week and offer their wares for sale. A new suit for a man would cost less than one pound. Boots and shoes would be five to ten shillings (25 to 50p) a pair. Workmen wore strong trousers of corduroy. In large families the younger children usually wore hand-me-downs, new clothes went to the oldest or the largest and then down through the family. Few of the younger children ever had anything brand new. Girls were luckier than the boys as dresses could be altered more easily and most mothers were extremely able with scissors and needles.

Many cottages in those days were very small, having just the one main room downstairs which was the kitchen-cum-dining room where all meals were cooked on an open fire and baking done on a side oven. Upstairs there were usually two small bedrooms. Many of these cottages were built against the steep hillside, with only small windows facing the front so that inside it was always gloomy darkness. The oil lamp was the main source of light and candles were used to light the way to bed. Few of these cottages had a water supply so water for all needs had to be carried from the village pump or from two natural springs at each end of the village. Toilet facilities were practically nil so that there were dry outside closets. It is surprising how large families were reared under such conditions but people happily survived.

Few houses had bathrooms, and each Saturday evening a tin bath, about three feet long and eighteen inches wide, was brought into the kitchen, put in front of the fire and then we would take turns to have our weekly bath, with knees tucked under our chins so that we fitted in. After each child emerged a kettle of hot water was added to the bath to warm it up for the next child.

In the winter months my mother would take the live embers from the fire and put them into a warming pan. Most homes had one of these but if not, a special brick would be warmed in the oven, wrapped in newspaper and placed in the bed. Some people used stone hot water bottles wrapped in nighties.

Cooking was done on the kitchen range but later we had gas stoves which proved an enormous help to busy housewives with many mouths to feed. On most fireplaces you would find a large iron saucepan into which bones would be put to be boiled clean. Onions, carrots and turnips were added to make a stew which lasted for days. This was known as the Welsh 'cawl'.

Large meals had to be prepared every day. For dinner the meat most commonly served was bacon or if an old hen refused to lay we had boiled fowl for a change. Roast or stewed rabbit made a cheap and appetising meal which helped to vary the diet. Fish was sometimes found on the menu. A favourite pudding was spotted dick, a roly-poly made with currants. The pudding was rolled in a greased pudding cloth tied at both ends like a sausage and boiled in the pot with the meat and the vegetables. Fruit tart or custard, tapioca, rice or sago pudding were usually served.

At a certain time of the year on the waxing of the moon, a pig which had been well fattened up was killed. The intestines were removed and rendered down to make delicious 'scratchings' which left behind the finest lard. Tasty faggots were made from the various organs, with the pig's fry, steaks and spare ribs being much sought after. Much of this was shared with neighbours who later returned the compliment. When the pig was cut up, the hams and shoulders were carried into an outbuilding or

The village pump and the village bellman, about 1890

cellar and laid on a stone slab. Saltpetre was rubbed into them and they were then covered with salt and left for about three weeks to cure. The salt was bought in large slabs and had to be cut up and crushed before use. At the appropriate time the hams and shoulders were wrapped in muslin bags and then hung from sturdy hooks in the kitchen rafters. Pork was a staple diet, but a sheep's head would also provide a good meal with the brains and the tongue all being used. Brawn was also very popular.

Butter was eaten only on Sundays and at other times bread was spread with dripping. Vegetables were plentiful, having been grown in the many cottage gardens.

All the clothes washing was done in the back kitchen. Here, in the corner, we had a large cast iron boiler which had to be filled early in the morning with clean water. A fire was then started under the boiler with an abundant supply of timber already put to one side to keep the fire going. Washing day was the worst day of the week, with clouds of steam and the smell of washing everywhere. The clothes were immersed in a large bath of hot soapy water to soak before being vigorously rubbed on the ribbed washing board. There were no detergents or washing powders and washing was done with a bar of yellow washing soap which contained a proportion of soda. As the clothes boiled they had to be constantly pushed down with a wooden handle to prevent the water from boiling over and sending up clouds of ash from the fire. After rinsing, the whites were finally bleached by squeezing a bag of Reckitt's Blue into the water.

The mangle and washing tub were much in use while the three-legged dolly took much effort in twisting and turning as it was heavy and awkward to use. Sometimes, to help keep the washing boiler going, I would take a sack and set off to the seashore hoping to find any pieces of driftwood that had been left by the tide. The full sacks would be carried home to augment our coal supplies. Sometimes we were lucky enough to find the odd pieces of coal. Land around the village, including the beach, was dotted with clothes posts with long lines used by the women-folk to hang out their washing to dry.

Should washing day turn out to be wet it was postponed until better weather but if bad weather persisted the job had to be done and the wet clothes were draped on clothes horses around the fire, filling the place with steam and making life thoroughly uncomfortable. Ironing was done on the kitchen table on a folded blanket. Flat irons heated against the bars of the grate were tested and if the iron was sufficiently hot it had to be carefully wiped with a damp cloth to remove all smoke and smuts. Iron holders were essential for the intensely hot handles.

Winter evenings were a time for the family to get together around a roaring coal fire to sing in harmony. Late one Sunday, the village deserted, a man was seen to be quietly standing in the middle of the square. He was identified as the village Squire and eventually he was hesitantly approached and asked if he required help of some kind. His reply was 'Listen to that wonderful singing.' On being told that it came from a humble cottage he said, 'That man, surrounded by his many children, is better off than I am with all my worldly wealth.'

Winter shadows appeared as the days closed in. Early darkness meant the return of the oil lamp which was filled with paraffin, the wick trimmed, the glass polished and put in the centre of the room on the kitchen table. At first the wick was turned up only slightly so as to warm the chimney gradually in order to prevent it cracking or becoming clouded by smoke. The honey-coloured light lit up the centre of the kitchen but barely reached the distant corners.

Although gas street lighting had appeared in the village in 1868, the lamp standards were far apart, leaving pockets of darkness in between the haloes of light, the weak glare of cottage candles, the beam of an occasional torch, the glow of a hurricane lantern or yellow light of a carbide bicycle lamp. At dusk the village lamplighter made his rounds, walking the length of the village with his long pole with which he would pull a small chain attached to each lamp. Later the gas lamps were fitted with a pilot light. Never again will we hear the tread of the lamplighter at close of day, nor will the new day be heralded by the sound of the milkman's horse. Such sounds are destined to reside only in the memory.

We sat at the table to play ludo, snakes and ladders, snap and draughts. Sometimes we were called upon to make spills from the weekly newspapers to be used for lighting candles and lanterns. In very cold weather we left our hobbies to join the semicircle around the fire, toasting the fronts of legs and faces while our backs were exposed to draughts from all quarters. As we knew no other we accepted these conditions and as healthy, unpampered children, barely noticed them. We looked for pictures in the fire, watched the firelight's reflection flecking the window panes and twinkling on the polished fender, while outside screeching winds lent to the hearth an added cosiness.

In those days, before radio and television, silences were broken only by the human voice, the cracking flames and the ticking clock. A neighbour dropping in with news or tales of bygone days was a welcome diversion. We children loved listening to these tales but knew better than to butt into the adults' conversation. Meanwhile, mother's fingers were constantly busy with darning, mending or knitting socks.

During the winter we were treated with blackcurrant tea for colds and goose-grease on hot brown paper was applied to tight chests. A spoonful of goose-oil was ideal for a raw throat or something warm tied around the neck with a woollen sock. Our cuts and abrasions were disinfected with iodine and soothed with

Zambuk or Germoline, while sprains and strains were rubbed with liniment or embrocation.

The first weeks in the spring brought the annual 'Spring Cleaning' ritual, very destructive to our home life. It was a period of unrelieved chaos, with scratch meals and the whole house disorientated. Every inch of every wall, floor, ceiling and all the contents had to be brushed, scrubbed, polished or painted, with chimneys swept. Before the days of vacuum cleaners, dust which had accumulated throughout the year was swept away.

All beds were filled with goose feathers. Bedmaking was a time-consuming job, for all beds had to be stripped and pummelled before being made up.

One by one, rooms were cleared of all movable articles, large heavy furniture was eased from the walls, ceilings and walls were brushed and more often than not papered or distempered. Cupboards and drawers were emptied, wiped out and relined with fresh paper, contents overhauled and useless stuff discarded. Crockery from dresser shelves and cupboards was washed. Everything was in confusion and everyone's life thrown out of joint. We all breathed a sigh of relief when life returned to normal and every room smelt sweet and clean.

The old and the new: Gas lighting (1868) and electric lighting (1945)

Most housewives were keen to keep their homes tidy and well run. Kitchen ranges were regularly black-leaded and every day there were special activities: washing on Monday, ironing on Tuesday, baking on Wednesday, bedrooms cleaned on Thursday and the living rooms on Friday. The weekend came to be enjoyed as a break from all chores, when the family came together, and people relaxed in their different ways before Monday came again to renew the rituals.

In the spring we were given tonics. First came internal cleansing with Senna tea, and how we detested that stuff! There was also Clarke's Blood Mixture to purify the blood. Then, to build us up, we were given brimstone and treacle, cod liver oil and malt, Scott's Emulsion and Virol, which were all unpleasant to take.

As children we were impressed with the need for thrift. We were encouraged to work and earn money, which was handed over to our mother and, in return, we received a very small part back as pocket money. How to spend this pocket money was always a problem; you had a pleasing quantity of sweets for a penny so the question was whether to spend everything at once or divide it out on half penn'orth of this and half penn'orth of something else. The 'something else' was the real problem, for the choice was between dolly mixtures, bulls-eyes, aniseed balls, liquorice allsorts, sherbet powder skilfully sucked up through a tube of liquorice, liquorice strings and packets of sugar cigarettes, with pink glowing ends. These treats each provided a glorious explosion of tastes so that the enticing local sweet shop was entered with a thrill of anticipation.

Householders anxious to supplement the family income took in paying guests who generally stayed for a fortnight or even longer. Some houses were vacated so that they could be let furnished for a whole month, generally in July and August. Boys camped on the land near the railway station, which is now a caravan site, thus making an extra bedroom available for visitors and providing additional income for the household. Some boys were employed during the summer season as messengers, delivering goods from local shops to the several boarding houses and hotels as well as to private houses.

Life was hard in those days for most people, but there was a great deal of mutual help, and there was a magnificent communal spirit. Country folk everywhere could read the signs which indicated that things were not well and very soon they knew exactly what had gone wrong. Sometimes a sudden illness in the family would make it virtually impossible to do all the necessary chores. The word went round and the neighbours would share the work out between them, establishing a kind of roster to ensure that whenever things became difficult the maximum help was always at hand. Indeed, help in different forms was often readily available.

EARLY VILLAGE LIFE

Within the village and during my childhood, tuberculosis was then one of the many serious illnesses and with no National Health Service, the doctor was called only when matters were serious and, unfortunately, often too late. Sometimes the doctor's bill would be settled by some gift or a service in lieu of money and sometimes he would 'forget' to send his bill to the very poor people of the village.

The Sunday School and Band of Hope were very well attended. The magic lantern shows, which had a powerful but smelly acetylene lights, showed slides which were owned by the Temperance Movement. They were used as a most effective visual aid to drive home the evils of strong drink. The Temperance Movement was very powerful in the village and anyone taking strong drink would be virtually ostracised.

We all sang the Temperance songs with gusto and verve. So, of course, we all signed the pledge. I signed at the early age of five and had difficulty holding the pen as before that I had always used a pencil. It was regarded, with christening, as part of the ritual which cleansed us from original sin. Confirmation was the complementary ritual in our early teens which protected us against its reappearance as a sort of topping up of the original inoculation. But, more important, you had to sign the pledge and wear white ribbons.

December was awaited with a lively and growing anticipation. At Christmas time the windows of shops were transfigured into an Aladdin's Wonderland. The effect on us was magical as we appeared as if from nowhere on the dark December evenings, squinting into the shop windows with the circle of upward-turned little faces reflecting the pink glow against the murky blackness behind us, for there were not many street lights then. There were toys of the most exotic and ingenious kind: clockwork toys with their keys at the side, books, paints, dolls and always a doll's pram. Row upon row of wonders were examined in detail from every angle in the days before Christmas: gauze stockings, paper hats, streamers, balloons, clay bubble pipes, shining metal puzzles, transfers, celluloid ducks and tin whistles, mouth organs, humbugs and chocolate coins, liquorice sweet cigarettes, sherbet, boxes of marbles with both plain and multicoloured glass, penknives, toy pistols firing off caps, torches and paint boxes. There were riches to fill everyone's imagination and endless Christmas lists.

Meccano, a new construction kit, now appeared, which appealed to the older boys as they could assemble various types of models, from cranes and bridges to cars and many more complicated models. Once a chosen design had been built and played with, it was dismantled and a fresh start made on a new subject. It was far more than a toy and most boys aspired to own a set. Those who could least afford one had to have set No. 00. Indeed, the number of the set was a very accurate indicator of the family's affluence. I won't reveal the number of my Meccano set, but I had great pleasure from it over the years.

Some of the boys had a steam engine which was worked by a small methylated lamp. Generally only the better-off families were able to afford these. Care had to be taken with the engines as their explosive mixtures could easily catch fire. The final scene of the madly revolving flywheel in its frenzied death throes, with molten lead flying off dangerously in all directions, was a sad moment for any young child.

In the two to three weeks before Christmas all the children in the village pinned their hopes and dreams on one article or another. There was no accounting for taste and there was no accounting for our choice. We decided what we wanted from the window and went back, from time to time, to see if it was still there. A kind of proprietary relationship developed between us and our heart's desires. Alas, when

Christmas came, many of us, probably most of us, were disappointed. The Hornby train set, the Meccano, the steam engine, oh well.... whatever it was we wanted was probably far beyond the resources of our parents and we had to make do with a more modest, often home-made gift. Meanwhile, our dreams of what might have been lingered on for a while but the willingness of each of us to share our toys made the deprivation easier to bear and there was always next Christmas when, perhaps, the dreams would come true.

As young children we had few toys and made our own fun. With makeshift things we were far happier than many children showered with expensive toys, easily come by and lightly valued. Our spontaneous play thoroughly absorbed and satisfied us.

We had a few comics and read magazines like the Boy's Own Paper and of course many homes had a set of Children's Encyclopaedias. There were other books available, such as 'Treasure Island', 'Tom Brown's Schooldays', 'Kidnapped', and 'Biggles' and the 'William' stories. These books added to our lively imaginations and spirit of adventure, all of which could be acted out on our beloved hills behind Aberdyfi or on its sandy shore. We could be instant pirates, castaways, or scruffy, meddlesome William characters. Aberdyfi gave us the perfect stage. We played endless games with toy soldiers. These were an echo of the military activity during 1914-1918 war and we could base our games on what we heard. Boyhood games could be boisterous, sometimes unruly and occasionally could lead to trouble with the village policeman. However, he was wise to many of our tricks and he had no difficulty in keeping us in order. Sometimes the punishment was on the spot and immediate, such as a ban from the area, a clip on the ears, a threat to tell parents, or the confiscation of a possession.

Discipline was strict and moral guidance readily passed on and instilled in us. We were brought up to be dutiful and obedient, to be trustworthy and honest whilst showing respect to our elders and courtesy to all around. We had no doubts as to what was acceptable or unacceptable. Parental decisions brooked no argument and any potential disobedience was immediately checked and suggestions of defiance or insolence were instantly reprimanded.

It was rare for parents to fail in such matters but if they did, problems in families often appeared later in life in some form. Of course, we sometimes resented the discipline as young people will always try to test a system but we invariably respected the disciplinarian and doubted those who wanted to disobey.

No child that I knew grew up with a police record. Violence and crime were practically non-existent and still had the power to shock and horrify. Dad was our family disciplinarian and when he was around we had to be on our best behaviour. He kept a small cane on top of the mantelpiece and if he had cause to speak more than once, a quick glance up at the mantelpiece with the enquiry, 'Where is the cane?' brought about the desired effect. There was never any need to bring it down.

Telephones were scarce in the village and public call boxes completely lacking. If a telephone was needed, which was not often, then a visit had to be made to the village Post Office.

Outside normal hours you had to knock at the door of the post-mistress's private flat above the office. Messages were conveyed to residents in the locality by children who received a penny for their services. When a telegram had to be delivered, the post-mistress opened the office and blew a whistle. The first child to answer the summons got the job and there was much competition. Serious messages relating to deaths and accidents at sea or in foreign parts were taken personally by the post-mistress, who very tactfully broke the news herself before handing over the cold missive.

My childhood was in an age when the gramophone was still a novelty, with its tin horn and wax cylinder. The machine had to be wound up by hand and, though the music sounded tinny, we all thought it was wonderful. The delicate tinkle of music boxes was also to be heard in many a home. Radio was of course in its infancy and television unknown, so if we wanted music we had to produce it for ourselves.

I remember the great excitement brought about by the annual visit from a travelling circus. It was given as much space as needed on our football field and the putting up of the big top never ceased to amaze us with all its poles and vast canvas. As a scout with memories of trying to erect a smaller tent, I could appreciate the skill which was required.

Most of the village took advantage of this once-a-year spectacular and marvelled at the trapeze artists, acrobats, jugglers, the strong man and, of course, the antics of the clowns. The splendidly dressed, red-coated Ringmaster made us feel that we were watching something which seemed larger than life and beyond our usual experience.

The atmosphere of laughter, cries of fear for dare-devil feats and appreciative applause mingled with the smell of the sawdust, the noise of the animals and the throbbing sounds of the brightly polished traction engines. As we walked home through the darkness, with the Dyfi estuary gently restless at our side, most of us secretly wished we could join the circus people and live their glamorous lives.

Occasionally, a man with a barrel organ would visit us, sometimes with a real live monkey, and we excitedly followed this free entertainment along the village street.

Periodically we also had visits by a street singer. This was usually a poor person, often out of work, who used to go around from village to village singing hymns or any other song that appealed to the singer or audience. People would throw the odd penny, which would be avidly picked up and then the street singer would go on his melodious way.

Tramps in ragged ill-fitting clothes and broken boots were a common sight in the village. Their skin was grimy with dirt and their long matted hair jutted out from their battered hats. They carried tins with wire handles and begged housewives to fill them with scalding tea. Some were ill-tempered, but on the whole they were reasonable people. One I remembered particularly as he was more or less a regular visitor. Paddy was an Irishman, as you can guess. Tall and quiet, he was quite well known and was helped in his travels with gifts of food. When Paddy died, his hideout was discovered about two miles from Machynlleth, where it was found that he had built an altar for his own private use.

Sometimes a gypsy woman arrived carrying a large basket on her arm, followed by a couple of ill-kempt children. She had a swarthy, weather-beaten skin, greasy plaited hair and large earrings. She always played up to the housewives, calling them pretty ladies and assuring them of good fortune provided they crossed her palm with silver. Her basket contained clothes pegs, papers of pins, tape, combs, ribbons and laces. She begged for food and clothing, painting a distressing picture of the life of the gypsy.

There were regular visits by the tinker, who mended kettles and pans, and the knife grinder to sharpen knives and scissors. The peddler also did his rounds, selling small items such as socks and stockings, handkerchiefs and ties, needles and thread with pins and elastic.

Every year a man on a bicycle festooned with strings of onions paid us a visit. He wore a beret which was traditionally worn by French peasants. As a Breton he had a smattering of the Welsh language so was able to sell his commodity to the villagers. Naturally he was known as Johnny Onions.

In the autumn the threshing machine arrived at the neighbouring hill farms and drew us like a magnet. We would watch, fascinated as half a dozen strong horses dragged the cumbersome machine from farm to farm. All the farms combined their labour force to bring in the harvest, this being the Welsh custom. It worked to everyone's advantage whilst also creating a solid communal spirit.

Our roads today are sometimes the subject of much criticism but vast improvements have taken place both in their construction and surfacing. I remember the tremendous chaos caused by resurfacing the main road through our village. Stones were laid by hand and covered with soil, which was then well watered and flattened with a steamroller. It was a messy job but much enjoyed by the lads who followed the water cart and the steamroller with its panting noise and slow progress.

Although Aberdyfi in those days had a piped water supply, during the summer months the source often ran dry. It was then that buckets and jugs were brought out to carry water from the village pump in the square. Here was a fine opportunity for us to earn the odd halfpenny by carrying buckets of water to Penhelig and other areas a long distance from the pump.

Aberdyfi's mackerel and herring fleet, manned and owned by retired seamen, put their sailing skills into events arranged at an Annual Regatta, when at the height of summer they engaged in keen competition with each other and with any would-be challengers to their sailing prowess who might have come from Barmouth or Aberystwyth. Regattas have always been popular in such a sea-orientated village as Aberdyfi, where so many were dependent upon the waters of the estuary or the wider sea beyond the bar. As early as 1880 there was a sailing regatta in Aberdyfi, but as the numbers of the old sea-faring community dwindled over the years, the sailing Regatta changed to Aquatic Sports, which proved to be very popular with the new generation.

With the decline in shipping, the men who once sailed the high seas to all corners of the earth were now ashore. To earn a livelihood, they turned their energies to fishing in Cardigan Bay, and net fishing for salmon in the upper reaches of the River Dyfi. I remember many boats, with the owner as skipper and a crew of two men, setting out to parts of the river that were regularly netted. Fishing went on both day and night according to the state of the tides. Sometimes catches were good, but when it was a poor season the outlook for the long winter ahead was bleak.

A familiar sight for us all were the nets spread out to dry on poles that were erected on the beach. Here you could often see men busily carrying out repairs to the nets and quietly reminiscing and telling their magical tales of the sea.

During summer months they hired their boats to visitors, some of whom, however, were unable to row. Though only some twelve to thirteen years of age at that time, I was familiar with the Dyfi and knew its varying moods, and so I was trusted to take boatloads of visitors up and down the river. There was no real danger to them, but care had to be continually exercised.

During the winter months many of these men turned their hand to mussel gathering. They scraped the bed of the river with rakes 15 to 18

Scraping the river bed for mussels, 1930

feet long. The mussels were put into sacks and dispatched to the Midland markets.

The Literary Institute then, as now, was in a wonderful situation for all village activities, being central and within easy reach for everyone. To stand at its bay window and look out to sea with an uninterrupted view of the estuary with one of the most peaceful vistas imaginable.

A religious sect, called the Plymouth Brethren, once held their meetings at the Institute. Built on the seashore, this building was then known as the Bath House, an appropriate name, as their teachings required that they made frequent use of total immersion. When this building was acquired by the inhabitants of Aberdyfi, it became the focal point for most of the village organisations for meetings, lectures, classes, a library and a reading room having daily newspapers with weekly and monthly publications, while billiards, snooker, chess and draughts were played. Gambling was not allowed and certainly no foul language.

Many of the older men would meet in a small room which was known as the House of Lords. Sitting around a coal fire, they discussed both national and local affairs. We boys were not allowed into this holy of holies.

As I had left school at the age of fifteen, which many did at that time, I realise now that I was a half-educated, self-opinionated and argumentative boy. However, I still subconsciously wanted to know more, and I went frequently to the library in the Literary Institute. Unfortunately, the choice of material was limited and although I did have some useful reading material it was somewhat restricted. When I heard about classes that were held at the Institute under the University of Wales Extra-Mural Department for Adult Education, I decided to go along to see what they could offer me. Here I found men and women of mature age, some of whom were politically reactionary, others atheist or agnostic, with some members of Church and Chapel. Many were deep thinkers, well read, but sometimes finding difficulty in expressing themselves.

The professor proved to be a man of wide education, with the ability to control his class and impart knowledge. I soon came to admire him and his skill and learnt a great deal from all the people involved. In fact, I think this is when I changed from adolescence to a degree of maturity with a firm footing in adult life.

A very flourishing Young People's Society met every Friday evening. It was non-sectarian and non-political. We had a formidable programme every winter, when papers on a variety of subjects were read, discussions on all sorts of topics took place and we had socials, concerts, impromptu speaking, debates and lectures. It was a first class breeding-ground for young people to become good citizens and at ease in conversation.

The village began to grow, albeit slowly. There was an increasing need for social events such as concerts and public meetings. It was realised that chapel vestries and the local school could not meet the needs of the numbers attending and a much larger building was required.

When in 1920 it was learnt that an army camp was being dismantled, a large wooden structure was obtained, taken down and transported to Aberdyfi to be erected in Penrhos.

It became a popular focal point for the village where lively entertainments were enjoyed, with excellent local talent displayed to the advantage of all concerned. Miniature eisteddfodau were held, usually known as Competitive Meetings, and only when you qualified in these competitions could you venture to the heady heights of an area eisteddfod. There could be between twenty to thirty boys and girls taking part in a particular age group section and a red rosette signified a win, as no money prizes were given. A blue rosette showed a second place and a yellow third. These rosettes were much sought after and became a source of great pride for many families. Choral singing played a significant part in our lives. Aberdyfi had some talented choirs for both mixed voices and children. Sadly the structure began to deteriorate and in 1957 the present building was erected on the same site and named Neuadd Dyfi.

This proved to be a building which seemed to inject new life into the already varied activities of the village. There was something to appeal to everyone, whether it was a concert, a drama performance, an eisteddfod or a cinema show.

The social occasions and meetings which occur in the day-to-day life of any community can be vitally important. This certainly is particularly true of smaller villages. The very closeness of people's lives usually means more sharing, more caring and more socialising. From the proximity and shared events often comes a tangible and strong village identity to the mutual benefit of everyone involved.

This has definitely been the case in Aberdyfi where people seemed to share lives together with a certain amount of ease, where neighbours were helped whenever possible and there was a coming together whenever the occasion arose for some festival or celebration.

The village carrier with his horse-drawn four-wheeled waggon before the coming of motor cars and lorries

Our village fire brigade was far removed from the efficient fire services of today. A few implements and hosepipes on a handcart were kept in a shed in the square. The brigade was made up of all the able bodied men of the village. When there was a fire they were summoned by the sound of a ship's foghorn which disturbed the whole village, especially when heard at night. Men, young and old, hurried to operate the handcart. I remember very clearly being one of a crowd dashing along New Street when one of the wheels of the cart came adrift and we all fell in a heap along with the meagre relics of our fire-fighting equipment.

A single-track railway along the side of the river and an old turnpike road that we called the main road were our links with the outside world. The village carter delivered parcels, crates and boxes from the railway station to the shops. There was also a 'horse-bus' which was used to convey passengers to and from the railway station.

Old seamen were often seen around the village. They walked with a rolling motion and they all wore thigh-length seaboots. Inside the boots they had two pairs of long woollen stockings. This was their everyday mode of dress, apart from Sundays of course.

They were great talkers and walkers, and were a kind of village senate who discussed exhaustively every event, every occurrence and any change in the status quo both in the village and in the outside world. They argued about every subject under the sun. Sometimes they paired up to walk up and down the seafront, ten paces forward and ten backwards, turning inwards together each time. This practice had been acquired from pacing the small quarter-deck of the ships on which they had sailed.

Our village community had its own pecking order. The Squire of the village, who lived in Plas Penhelig, was at the apex, as one might expect, and he was the president of several organisations in the village, except of course those connected with Temperance or Chapel. Every boy had to touch his forelock to him. Leadership in our community also came from people who cared for the place. They accepted the responsibility for keeping it in a state of order and tidiness, and also gave of their time and ideas to generate village activities and therefore a sense of community.

In my lifetime I have witnessed the transition from the horse and cart days of my childhood through the railway age into the era of jet propulsion, the atomic bomb and space travel.

The horse-bus used to convey passengers to and from the railway station

When aeroplanes appeared it was such a rare and remarkable sight that people gathered in crowds to watch the phenomenon, something we now take very much for granted.

The coming of the car and the wireless inevitable produced a world which could not leave the old order unscathed.

With the development of the motor industry, the first motor car made its appearance in Aberdyfi. It conjured up an air of adventure, with plenty of noise, smoke, fumes and much snorting and vibrating. The starting handle was an essential piece of equipment, while windscreen wipers had not yet been invented. A large rubber bulb blew the horn to warn all and sundry of the car's erratic journey along the narrow Aberdyfi roads.

Motor cars were now appearing in increasing numbers on the main road in our village. Indeed, they could be seen almost every day by the beginning of the 1920s and collecting numbers was becoming a major schoolboy pastime. Some of the older folk, however, still believed that cars were just a passing fashion and that the horse would never be replaced. Few of us had ridden in a motor car, but when I was given an opportunity, I thought it was marvellous. It was draughty sitting in the back seat travelling along the twisting roads which were more suitable for horses than cars but the thrill of speed was remarkable.

Then the wireless brought the world to our village. In the beginning only a few houses had a set, which was of quite primitive construction. When I heard that someone had a set near my home, I went along there filled with curiosity. I was soon spotted, but much to my surprise, instead of being told to go away, I was handed an earpiece and invited to listen. On being asked if I could hear something I replied with an air of wonderment, 'Yes, music!' I was told that it was an orchestra and that the music came all the way from London: this was something beyond belief.

That was my first experience of sound radio. Small delicate receivers, called 'crystal sets', now began to appear, many having been assembled by skilled ex-army wireless operators. About 1918, a radio station was set up near Tywyn; I remember the towering masts upon the tops of the Merioneth hills.

Signor Marconi, in his immaculate steam yacht 'Electra', cruised into Cardigan Bay, carrying out experiments in communication between the yacht and the station. When the yacht berthed alongside the outer jetty, Marconi and his crew of young, good looking Italians, were made very welcome in the village.

During the early part of this century, Aberdyfi was a quiet, sleepy village and it was not until the period of the Second World War that once again it became a busy place and the river a hive of activity. Amphibious craft, a type of vehicle that had not been seen before, crossed and recrossed the estuary with ease. An important experimental station was set up on the south bank of the river, and day after day the sound of heavy gunfire shook the village. A barrage balloon unit was in operation and fast R.A.F. launches were berthed in the harbour and made daily sorties into Cardigan Bay. The area was also used for the training of commandos, who spent days and nights in the surrounding mountains, gaining experience for their undercover operations.

The people of the village responded to the calls of war by collecting large quantities of sphagnum moss, a plant which was required for medical purposes. Many women were involved in knitting articles for the use of the Armed Forces, as well as the collection of waste paper and bottles. Indeed, anything which could but used in the war effort was amassed in large quantities.

With the formation of the Home Guard men became very much involved and felt that they could make an important contribution. Many are the stories told about their activities and they are as humorous as those portrayed on television in the ever-popular programme, 'Dad's Army'.

The Second World War brought many evacuees from the vulnerable industrial areas to the countryside. Aberdyfi received its full quota, and as the children required school accommodation to continue their interrupted studies, the church, or National School was placed at their disposal while all the local children occupied the Board School.

So the middle part of the 1900s saw a return to an earlier bustle which was perhaps only to be seen again as the tourist industry grew and visitors to Aberdyfi increased in the latter years of the century.

ABERDYFI WHARF AND LEISURE AREA

It is difficult for the casual observer sitting on the jetty today, perhaps watching the boys and girls from the Outward Bound School carrying out various activities, or yachts sailing peacefully by in the estuary, to imagine the very different scene it would have been in the sixteenth and seventeenth centuries.

The principal occupation at that time was fishing, and small craft would be off-loading their catch of herring and mackerel, which were in plentiful supply. These boats would be out in Cardigan Bay in all weathers in order to learn their hard way of living. However, with the Industrial Revolution, the late eighteenth century saw the rapid growth of Aberdyfi as a port with ships sailing to all parts of the world.

As Aberdyfi adapted to the necessary changes, fishing was more and more superseded by boat-building skills. Between 1840 and 1880 no fewer than 45 ships were built here and visitors can still see signs of the shipyards and particularly the massive mooring rings fixed to the sea-wall. The large anchors also noticeable on the foreshore show that the ships must have been of considerable size.

The value of Welsh slate, which is unrivalled anywhere in the world and still in demand, was appreciated at this time and quarries were opened at Corris, Abergynolwyn and Aberllefenni. Aberdyfi was the natural port to which this slate was transported to be shipped in the large vessels accommodated in the harbour.

This busy trade rapidly brought about the need for a wharf and one was erected in 1882. Fortunately, some 15 years earlier, railway facilities had been completed, so Aberdyfi was able to cope with the new trading demands.

Aberdyfi now became a bustling scene with ships being loaded with slate from the wharf by gangs of men who also off-loaded timber from Newfoundland and the Baltic, with railway sleepers for the further extension and maintenance of the railway. Coal and potatoes were also landed here in some quantity.

Built the same time as the wharf, a jetty was erected so that ships could load and unload whatever the state of the tide. This jetty had to support a double track of railway lines and a large turntable, so it had to be strongly built. There were three landing stages, the highest one having railway lines which connected it with the main line at Aberdyfi railway station. By building the other two landing stages at

Deterioration of wharf structure

different levels it was possible for cattle, pigs and horses to walk ashore from the ships into special pens erected along the front of Glandovey Terrace. From here they were loaded into cattle trucks to be transported away by rail.

However, the coming of the railway heralded the decline of shipping and the steam engine proved to be a fatal blow to the old sailing ships. Gradually shipbuilding and then shipping itself decreased, and during the early part of the 20th century only a few steamers still came to Aberdyfi.

During the years following the 1914–18 War, there was little commercial acivity in the Aberdyfi area; the pier became silent and the once busy wharf was used as a coal dump. There was a short flurry of activity when ships arrived with cargoes of cement for construction work at Lake Vyrnwy for Liverpool Corporation's water works and later for the Birmingham Corporation at the Elan Valley Reservoirs. When these large schemes were completed the harbour became once again very quiet, and over the years the structure of the wharf and jetty steadily deteriorated. It was feared that a severe storm might cause extensive damage or even partial collapse of the structure.

The wharf area became dilapidated, untidy and unkempt and was the cause of much embarrassment to the many people who were anxious to develop Aberdyfi as a seaside resort. Protracted discussions and negotiations ensued which eventually allowed the Council to proceed with several schemes for the development and improvement of the area. Most important was the building of new public toilets. The work was completed in October 1968 at a cost of £52,360.

The wharf repair was a major scheme whose final cost was almost £50,000. Extensive jetty repairs had been done in 1968 and then it was discovered that the Teredo worm had infested the timber piles. While the timber looked sound on the surface, internally it had been eaten by this marine borer and it was realised that the jetty was on the verge of imminent collapse. A new jetty had to be constructed at a cost of £28,242. At the same time the old wharf buildings, occupied and used by the Outward Bound School, were repaired and renovated.

An Information Centre for the Snowdonia National Park was part of the final building phase together with a public shelter, the Harbourmaster's Office and a new Clubhouse for the Dyfi Sailing Club, with gardens and leisure area.

Gardens and leisure area, 1972

Thus over a period of eight years from the date of its purchase, this whole area was transformed. With seats, flowers and shrubs given by the many admirers of Aberdyfi, the scene presented at the Official Opening on the 28th September, 1972, was truly memorable.

In November 1972, the council was informed that 'the clearing of a derelict area in the centre of the village to create a fine new amenity had been considered worthy of a Prince of Wales Award for Environmental Improvement'.

THE UNKNOWN WARRIORS

Hitler's accession as German Chancellor in 1933 and the subsequent invasion of Austria produced a flood of refugees from Germany, Austria and other European countries. Many came to Britain. Among them were young men, keen to play a part in the defeat of the Nazis and their evil government.

However, when war broke out in 1939, these refugees were still technically enemy aliens, and their loyalty to the Allied cause was ignored. So when Hitler's armies invaded the Low Countries and England's south coast was threatened, refugees living in the south-east of the country were interned as a precautionary measure.

When the danger of invasion had passed and no spies had been discovered among the refugees, they were released and at last given the chance to contribute to the war effort. At first their only option was to join the unarmed Pioneer Corps. Then, in 1942, a special opportunity arose.

On the recommendations of Earl Mountbatten, then Chief of Combined Operations, Churchill personally authorised the formation of a Commando Troop wholly consisting of loyal enemy aliens. Its members were to be used singly or in small groups as front-line soldiers on missions of all kinds, or as intelligence personnel, for which their linguistic skills made them uniquely valuable.

Over three hundred and fifty young refugees volunteered for unspecified dangerous duties with this new Commando Troop, which was to be known as 3 Troop, 10 (IA) Commando. Initially eighty-six men were hand-picked by Major Hilton-Jones MC, a Welshman from Caernarfon, who was to command the unit.

Many members of the Troop were of Jewish ancestry, but religion or background were definitely not the criteria for membership. The lucky ones were chosen for their fluency in German, their aptitude for initiative and self-reliance and their potential as elite troops. In order to prevent German intelligence from discovering the existence of the Troop, and to protect as far as possible each individual in the event of capture, each man was given a British name and a fictitious identity.

In their new disguise the members of 3 Troop arrived in Aberdyfi in the autumn of 1942. They received a wonderful welcome from the people of the village; the landladies with whom they were billeted still remember them with

The monument in Penhelig Park

genuine affection.

The commandos underwent rigorous training for a period of some nine months. They pounded the roads for miles around the village, climbed Cader Idris and Snowdon and were plunged into the cold waters of the Dyfi in their pursuit of fitness. Meanwhile the 'Smiths' and 'Joneses' of 3 Troop were being taught how to bomb and shoot. They learned how to survive in enemy terrain by stealth, how to interrogate prisoners, and how the Wehrmacht and its weaponry worked. Before the war ended, each commando had taken part in one or more assignments in most theatres of the war.

From 1942 onwards, the men disappeared in twos and threes on secret missions over France. They were dropped by night off the coast, or were parachuted into the country to gather information and to contact agents.

For most of them, however, first blood was to be D-Day itself. In the first assault, three troopers died on the Normandy beach, and within days several more would perish. By May 1945, one in four of the commandos were dead, half of them were wounded (at least once), and some had been tortured. But they had raided occupied France, fought their way up through Italy, been on the D-Day beaches and penetrated beyond the lines during the Allied advance into Germany itself.

Half a century on, the survivors from those terrible days returned to Aberdyfi from America, New Zealand, Germany, Canada and England. On the morning of Saturday 15th May 1999, twenty-two of the survivors gathered, with their children and grandchildren in the sun on a rocky spot on the edge of the village. In a simple and moving ceremony, they unveiled a slate monument bearing the inscription:

> 'For the members of 3 Troop 10 Commando, who were warmly welcomed in Aberdyfi while training for special duties in battle. Twenty were killed in action.'

Brian Grant, a former member of the Troop, now aged eighty-two and a retired judge, who was Chairman of the Monument Committee, has summed up the feelings of the survivors in these words:

> 'We regard Aberdyfi as the place of our rebirth. After years of discrimination, persecution and second-class citizenship, membership of 3 Troop enabled us to participate fully in the defeat of Hitler and to establish ourselves in the post-war world as equal naturalised citizens of the Free World'.

VILLAGE ACHIEVEMENTS

1972 Prince of Wales Award for Environmental Improvement in Aberdyfi
Presentation by H.R.H Prince Charles at Denbighshire Technical College
1973 Winners Best kept Village
Winners Wales in Bloom
Finalist Britain in Bloom
Presentation by Sir Alexander Glen, Chairman of the British Tourist Authority, at a special
　reception in Martini Terrace, London
1974 Winners Best Kept Village
1976 Winners Best Kept Village
Presentation by Mr Barry Jones, M.P., Minister in Charge of Tourism, Welsh Office, at Bangor
　Normal College
1977 Winners Best Kept Village
Winners Wales in Bloom
Presentation by Mr Ednyfed Hudson Davies, Chairman of the Wales Tourist Board, at Swansea
　Leisure Centre
Finalist Britain in Bloom
　Presentation by Mr Henry Marking, Chairman of the British Tourist Authority, in London
1978 Winners Best Kept Village
Winners Wales in Bloom
Presentation at Aberystwyth by Sir Goronwy Daniel, Principal of the University College of Wales
Winners Britain in Bloom
Presentation by Lord Aberconway, President of the Royal Horticultural Society, at the Royal
　Festival Hall, London
Bronze medal in the 'Entente Florale' Competition between Britain, Belgium and France
Presentation by Mr F. Doerflinger of the International Flower-Bulb Centre
1979 Winners Best Kept Village
Winners Wales in Bloom
Presentation by Mr Tom Ellis, M.P., at the Plas Madoc Leisure Centre, Wrexham
Finalist Britain in Bloom
Presentation by Mrs Alison Munro on behalf of the British Tourist Authority at the Cafe Royale,
　London

WELCOME...

Discover Google's hidden tools

We all know that Google is a fantastic search engine. If we want to find something online, it's the first place most of us visit. But the search giant has dozens of other superb sites and services to enhance our experience online. Let's face it – if you're not using Google properly, then you're not using the web properly.

In this book we've highlighted tips to make the most of Google's best secret features – 267 of them, to be exact. It's an essential guide to getting more from Google, exploring its cutting-edge services and life-enhancing sites, revealing hidden tools that all web enthusiasts will want to know. We've lifted the lid on all of Google's must-use services, from Gmail to Street View, Google+ to Chrome, revealing expert ways to unlock their full potential. You'll discover how Google can improve your website, boost your security online and speed up your web browsing – plus much, much more. You'll also learn incredible tips for Android, Google's smartphone operating system, and find out which tablet PC you should buy.

If you love the web, then you can't afford to be in the dark about Google's hidden tools. Without the tips and tricks in this book, you'll only be using the internet in third gear.

Daniel Booth, Editor
daniel_booth@dennis.co.uk

THE ULTIMATE GUIDE TO GOOGLE'S HIDDEN TOOLS

EDITORIAL

Editor
Daniel Booth

Art Editor
Natalie Florey

Production
Rob Woodcock

COVER ILLUSTRATION
lewing@isc.tamu.edu

PHOTOGRAPHY
Danny Bird, Jan Cihak, Pat Hall, Timo Hebditch, Andrew Ridge
Digital Production Manager
Nicky Baker

MANAGEMENT

MagBooks Publisher
Dharmesh Mistry

Publishing Director
John Garewal

Operations Director
Robin Ryan

Managing Director of Advertising
Julian Lloyd-Evans

Newstrade Director
David Barker

Chief Operating Officer
Brett Reynolds

Group Finance Director
Ian Leggett

Chief Executive
James Tye

Chairman
Felix Dennis

MAGBOOK
The 'MagBook' brand is a trademark of Dennis Publishing Ltd, 30 Cleveland St, London W1T 4JD.
Company registered in England. All material © Dennis Publishing Ltd, licensed by Felden 2011, and may not be reproduced in whole or part without the consent of the publishers.

ISBN 1-907779-45-0

LICENSING/SYNDICATION
To license this product, please contact Hannah Heagney on +44 20 7907 6134, email hannah_heagney@dennis.co.uk. For syndication queries, please contact Anj Dosaj-Halai on +44 20 7907 6132, email Anj_Dosaj-Halai@dennis.co.uk

LIABILITY
The publishers cannot be held responsible for the accuracy of information in this MagBook or any consequence arising from it. Dennis Publishing takes no responsibility for the companies advertising in this MagBook.

The paper used within this MagBook is produced from sustainable fibre, manufactured by mills with a valid chain of custody.

Printed by BGP, Bicester, Oxon

Google, the Google logo and other devices are trademarks or service marks of Google. The Ultimate Guide To Google's Hidden Tools is an independently produced guide, and is not affiliated with, nor has it been authorised, sponsored, endorsed or otherwise approved by Google.

CONTENTS: The Ultimate

Chapter 1
What's new in Google

Control your social
   network with Google+ 6
15 Google blogs to read 8
Samsung Series 5 Chromebook 10
Build your own
   Google Chromebook 14

Chapter 2
Google's best add-ons

Google Docs 19
Picasa 21
iGoogle 22
Google Reader 23

Chapter 3
Secret search tips

Google's improved
   search features 28
Smarter and
   faster Google searches 30
Remove junk search results 32
Advanced tips for
   Google Desktop Search 33

Chapter 4
Get more from Chrome

Best new Chrome add-ons 36
Install and manage
   Chrome extensions 40
Tighten up Chrome's security 41

Chapter 5
Google Earth and Maps

Best Google Maps for holidays 44
12 secrets for
   Google Street View 46
Geolocate your photos
   in Google Earth from Picasa 48
Customise a Google Map 49
Combine Ordnance
Survey maps with Google 50
Create your own Google
   Earth video 52

Chapter 6
Use Gmail better

Unlock Gmail's hidden tools 56
Secret Gmail tips and tricks 58
Top 10 Gmail add-ons 65
Back up Gmail to
   your hard disk 67

Guide to Google's Hidden Tools

Gmail shortcuts..................... 68
Move your Hotmail
   account to Gmail..................... 69

Chapter 7
Make Google more secure

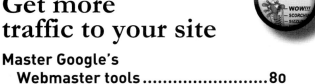

Make your Google
profile private.....................72
Protect your Google
account from hackers 73
Share photos privately
   with Picasa 74
How to keep everything
private in Google 75

Chapter 8
Get more traffic to your site

Master Google's
   Webmaster tools.....................80
Giving your website
   the local touch 84

Chapter 9
Top Android tips and tricks

Essential Android apps 88
Better browsing in Android 92

Fix Android problems 94
Make your own Android apps 96

Chapter 10
Product tests

How we tested the tablets 104
Acer Iconia Tab A500.................... 105
HTC Flyer 106
Asus Eee Pad Transformer 108
Samsung Galaxy Tab 10.1...............110
LG Optimus Pad 3D 112
Motorola Xoom........................... 114
Advent Vega...............................115
Dell Streak 115
Creative Ziio 7in 115
ViewSonic ViewPad 10s 115

Chapter 11
Google workshops

Use Google to manage your bookmarks
   online..118
Use Google Calendar's
   advanced features 121
Display your photos
   as a YouTube slideshow 122
Use Google Sites to
   create a free family website 124

Google A-Z 126
Google games............... 128

Chapter 1

What's new in Google

Control your social network with Google+ 6

15 Google blogs to read 8

Samsung Series 5 Chromebook 10

Build your own Google Chromebook 14

Control your social network with Google+

Love it or hate it, social networking is here to stay. Facebook is the largest social website, but it has a clunky interface that's riddled with quirks. Nevertheless, persuading its 750 million users to move elsewhere will be a gargantuan task.

Recently launched, but already boasting millions of users, Google+ is the search giant's latest attempt to put its stamp on social networking. It implements many of the improvements suggested by users of Facebook and Twitter, boasts a vastly superior interface and introduces the concept of separating your contacts into different social circles so you can control who sees what about you. For example, you can share a risqué photo of a stag weekend with your friends, but keep it from your work and family circles.

With group video chatting, and unlimited photo and video storage (as long as photos are smaller than 2,048 x 2,048 pixels, and videos shorter than 15 minutes), there's a lot of reasons why Google+ could be the next big thing.

ABOUT GOOGLE+

At the time of writing, you have to know someone on Google+ to get an invite, though we're expecting the service to open up to everyone soon. Sending invites is easy, as there's an 'Invite people to join Google+' link on every page. You will need a Google account to sign in, though. Get one from www.google.com/accounts.

1 The first thing to do is take control of your profile. Click the Profile button, **1** select About **2** and Edit Profile. **3** Select an option and type a description. **4** Click the down arrow **5** to control who can see it, then Save.

2 Circles are the key element of Google+. Click the Circles button **1** to manage them. You can create a new circle by dragging a contact's tile **2** to the grey circle, or hover your mouse over it and click 'Create circle'.

3 Hover your mouse over a circle to see who's in it. Click the circle for more options. You can rename it, **1** delete it **2** or add a new person. **3** To see the Circle members' updates, click 'View stream for this circle'. **4**

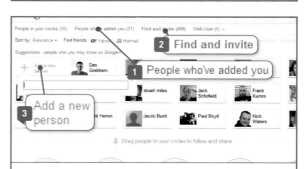

4 To find new people to link to, select 'People who've added you' **1** or 'Find and invite'. **2** Your Gmail contacts will be listed. Click 'Add a new person' and type a name or email to find unlisted people. **3**

EXPERT TIP

If you've got a webcam, try Google+ Hangouts, which lets you hold a video conference with the people in your circles. Click the green 'Start a hangout' button and install the software. Choose a circle and Google+ will send them a message. If you want a private chat, make a special circle with one person in it. The main screen switches to whoever is talking, or you can watch YouTube together.

5 You may find yourself being followed by people you don't know. If you don't reciprocate by putting them in one of your circles, they will only be able to see your public posts. See if they're worth following back by clicking Incoming. **1**

6 Likewise, if you're interested in someone else's public posts, don't be shy of putting them in your Following circle. **1** You can then read their public posts **2** and comment on them **3** if you wish.

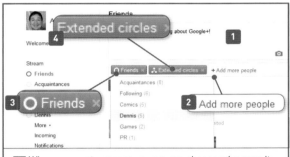

7 When you post a message, you can choose who sees it. Type your message **1** and click '+ Add more people'. **2** Blue buttons **3** indicate that the group is controlled by you. Green buttons **4** may be visible to strangers.

8 Once published, you can further control your message from the drop-down menu on the right. **1** You can edit and delete the post **2** and 'Disable comments'. **3** 'Disable reshare' **4** removes the Share link. **5**

9 You can also drag and drop photos and videos into the Stream box. Cut and paste a link from a website and Google+ will collect a synopsis of information from the site. **1** You can choose an appropriate picture with the arrows. **2**

10 Click your name, **1** then 'Account settings' **2** and Google+. **3** Phone alerts aren't available to UK members yet, but you can select email notification for a range of options.

15 Google blogs to read

Google's official blogs are must-read sites if you want to know about the company's latest releases. Here are 15 of the best

Analytics
http://analytics.blogspot.com

Google Analytics is the search giant's own site-monitoring service, providing you with the tools and information you

need to see who's visiting your site. This blog also contains loads of advice on getting the most from the service.

Android Developers
http://android-developers.blogspot.com

Packed with essential code and tips, this is a crucial read for all Android developers. Use the Tags column on the right-hand side for posts about specific versions of Android.

Blogger
http://buzz.blogger.com

If you use Blogger, this blog will help you get more from the service's tools. The archive stretches back to 2005.

Chrome
http://chrome.blogspot.com

With Chrome reinventing itself so frequently, it's no surprise that the browser's official blog is one of Google's busiest. Bookmark it for a heads-up on how the browser is evolving.

Docs
http://googledocs.blogspot.com

It's not always easy to master some of the advanced tools in Docs, so we're pleased that the official blog explains how to use them in crystal-clear English. You'll find tips on all the functions in Docs, including advice for spreadsheets and help on using the service on phones.

Gmail
http://gmailblog.blogspot.com

You'll find loads of useful tips and tricks from the Gmail team on this blog. Look out for the 'Faces of Gmail' feature, which is a Q&A with members of the Gmail staff.

Google+
http://googleplusplatform.blogspot.com
Reading the Google+ blog (above) is a great way to get to grips with the social network. If you're a Facebook veteran wondering whether or not you should switch, the tips here might persuade you.

Green
http://googlegreenblog.blogspot.com
Google's Green Blog is used to highlight the company's efforts to become more environmentally friendly. It's impressive to see how seriously they take the subject of saving energy.

Lat Long
http://google-latlong.blogspot.com
The Lat Long blog, updated almost every day, is where the Google Earth and Maps team celebrate new projects, tools and features. To find new places around the world to visit, look out for the Imagery Update posts.

Mobile
http://googlemobile.blogspot.com
Google's Mobile blog lets you know more about how the company's sites and services are being optimised, so they can be enjoyed on the move. Android fans should definitely bookmark it.

Search
http://insidesearch.blogspot.com
We all rely on Google for fast and relevant search results, so this blog is a fascinating glimpse into how the company tries to improve the service. Some of the best posts are the complicated ones, when the team explain about changes to site ranking and the all-important algorithm.

Security
http://googleonlinesecurity.blogspot.com
Google's Security blog gives you valuable tips on staying safe online, and reports on how the company is fighting the increasingly potent threat of web malware.

SketchUp
http://sketchupdate.blogspot.com
If you love creating 3D models in Google Earth, you'll find loads of inspiration in the official blog. Whenever new buildings are released for a city, you can watch stunning videos showing what's possible.

Translate
http://googletranslate.blogspot.com
Available to read in dozens of languages, from Afrikaans to Yiddish, the Translate blog explains how Google is helping to make the web a multi-lingual experience. You'll learn tips on better translation online, and discover which new languages Google is working with.

YouTube UK
http://youtube-global.blogspot.com
Had your fill of cute cats and giggling babies? Then visit the YouTube blog to find something new to watch. It does lean heavily towards US content, so you may prefer the UK-specific version of the blog at http://youtubeukblog. blogspot.com.

Samsung Series 5 Chromebook

PRICE £349 (Wi-Fi), £399 (3G and Wi-Fi); see box (left) SUPPLIER www.amazon.co.uk

Samsung's Chromebook promises a revolution in browsing using a web-based operating system, but does it deliver?

With the launch of the Samsung Chromebook, Google is claiming that the web-based Chrome operating system is a revolution in browsing. As laptops are mostly used for getting online, the search giant has shed the superfluous paraphernalia of a traditional operating system. Gone are the Desktop, program files and file managers in favour of a simpler browser-based system designed around being online at all times.

Google suggests that there isn't any offline function or software that you can't find an online alternative to. It's a bold move, but can it actually be practical, and is the Samsung Series 5 Chromebook a viable alternative to a netbook or tablet?

When it comes to features, the Chromebook has only one – the internet. The focus is on what it doesn't have, namely, a traditional operating system like Windows, Linux or Mac OS X. This means that there's no need to install updates – the Chromebook is always automatically up to date – and malware can't infect your PC by targeting out-of-date software. Traditional malware that's designed to target your hard drive and steal information from your PC cannot physically work on the Chromebook because hardly anything is kept on it.

All data stored on a Chromebook is encrypted and Google has security measures in place to protect your data in the cloud. It also uses 'sandboxing', which isolates apps and tabs, so if one gets infected, the malware won't spread to the whole machine. Should your Chromebook fail, it has a built-in Restore button that sends it back to the last-known healthy state. Because all your files are stored online, the restore won't affect them.

Online in 10 seconds

After you've pressed the On button, it takes the average laptop 45 seconds to get online – even longer if it's an older model. This is mainly because the operating system takes a while to load. Samsung claims the Chromebook takes less than 10 seconds to boot, although we managed to get online within eight seconds. If you close the lid to put it into Standby and reopen it again, you're back online within two seconds and video playback begins immediately. The only thing that takes any time at all is typing your Google password.

To get online, you need a Google account. This provides access to all your bookmarks, history and Google data, including anything else you already have set up on your PC's version of Google's Chrome browser. Alternatively, you can sign in using Guest Mode, which is the equivalent of launching an Incognito session in Chrome – perfect if you never want to store anything on your Chromebook or you are lending it to someone else.

The 12.1in screen is bright and perfect for streaming video, impressive even in HD. The full-size keyboard's flat keys make typing easy and it's been designed to be more web-friendly by replacing the traditional function keys with Back, Forward, Refresh and Volume, while Caps Lock has been replaced by a Google search key. The alphabet is printed on the keyboard in lower case and the whole of the oversized trackpad can be used for left-clicking, which makes it comfortable to use and speeds up browsing.

Offline drawbacks

The interface looks identical to the Chrome browser. Network connections are managed by right-clicking the signal bars in the top-right corner, and all the settings can be found by clicking the spanner icon underneath. We were expecting it to be crash-proof, but that didn't prove to be the case. During our tests the Wi-Fi connection went down a couple of times and we occasionally had to reboot, either because the operating system crashed completely or an error message appeared saying it had run out of memory – this, with only six tabs open.

If you haven't got access to an internet connection, the Chromebook's appeal is all but lost. There are over 600 offline apps in the Chrome Web Store, but simple omissions like a calculator (you won't realise how much you miss it until it's gone) are noticeable. Google Gears, the offline version of Google tools including Gmail and Docs, was removed from Chrome 12, so you can't work on documents or manage email offline anymore. Google has announced plans to offer offline versions of all its apps

in the summer, but that won't help early Chromebook purchasers. Not having a built-in hard disk means it's impossible to download software that doesn't have a web alternative. Downloading BBC iPlayer content, for example, needs storage, so you can stream it but can't save. Similarly, there's nowhere to store the Microsoft Silverlight downloads, which is used on Sky Player, among other sites.

The Chromebook has a small file manager for content taken from the web or for managing external storage devices, but its usefulness is kept to a minimum to encourage you to use the cloud. Plus, there's no browser ▶

choice. If a site works best on Firefox, or you normally use different browsers for different tasks, you won't have the option on a Chromebook.

Twice the price of a netbook

The Series 5's size and weight make it less portable than other netbooks, and it's certainly not as slick as a tablet. The saving grace, however, is its battery performance. Samsung claims the battery lasts 'all day' (around eight hours), and that video playback should last five hours. We didn't manage either of these, but just short of six-and-a-half hours for general use and four hours for video playback is still impressive.

With netbooks available for as little as £150, the Chromebook is twice the price for what feels like half the usability and features. It's priced at a similar level to most tablets but lacks that device's easy portability. To be permanently online, you'll have to pay the extra £50 for the 3G model with a data plan on top. All Chromebooks come with 3GB of data from Three (www.three.co.uk), which can be used in the first three months. After this time, or if you reach the 3GB limit before the three months is up, you have a choice of tariffs paid on a pay-as-you-go basis (see box on page 10).

Our verdict

The Chromebook, based on the browser that gives the device its name, feels instantly familiar and its web-centred design makes it easy to get online. However, its launch at a time when Google's offline functions are in limbo – Google Gears is gone and offline apps won't be around until later in the summer – is a big gamble for an online service. It feels like an overpriced prototype that exists primarily to push the Chrome operating system – stranded between netbook and tablet, without the affordability, convenience and usability of either. It might be worth waiting until the offline apps launch or Acer's Chromebook, which promises to be smaller, lighter and £50 cheaper, hits the shelves.

OVERALL ★★★★☆

PERFORMANCE ★★★★★
BATTERY LIFE ★★★★★☆
FEATURES & DESIGN ★★★★★★
VALUE FOR MONEY ★★★★★

ALTERNATIVES

Acer Aspire One D255 £250
http://bit.ly/acer270

Samsung Galaxy Tab £330
http://bit.ly/tab270

SPECIFICATION

12.1in (1,280 x 800) display, 1.5kg, Intel Atom dual-core processor, built-in dual-band Wi-Fi and world-mode 3G (optional), HD webcam, 2 x USB 2 ports, 4-in-1 memory-card slot, Mini-VGA port, full-sized Chrome keyboard

PROS Extremely accessible and familiar, and very fast to boot

CONS Little offline content, overpriced for the features available

CONTACTS
www.samsung.com/uk

Business
Step 1

Trading
Step 2 .biz

Register your .biz domain at Blacknight

Build your own Google Chromebook

Chrome OS is an operating system that Google has developed, based entirely around its Chrome browser. The main concept behind it is that you can do most of the things you currently do on your computer on the web instead. You don't need all that hard disk space to store your applications and data. Instead, you can use web apps like Gmail and Google Docs, which store everything in the cloud on their own servers. You don't have to back up your data, because it's already stored securely elsewhere, and because very little is stored on your computer, there are fewer security problems like viruses.

You can buy a new computer with Chrome OS already installed. We reviewed the Samsung Chromebook on p10. However, if you don't want a new computer, you can try Chrome OS out on your current PC, without making any permanent changes to it. All you need is a 2GB or bigger USB memory drive to run it from.

ABOUT CHROME OS
Launched by Google in 2009, Chrome OS has only recently made its way onto PCs. However, because the operating system is open source, anyone can download and try to run it on their own PC. An internet philanthropist known as Hexxeh has made a working version of the OS available on his website at http:// chromeos.hexxeh. net, which is the version we'll use in this workshop.

1 Get the latest version from http://bit.ly/chromeos274. To run the software from a USB memory drive, choose the USB option. **1** There's also a VirtualBox option **2** if you want to run it within Windows (see Step 10).

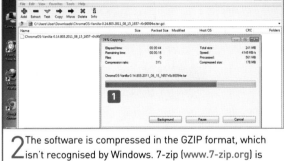

2 The software is compressed in the GZIP format, which isn't recognised by Windows. 7-zip (www.7-zip.org) is small, free and will decompress the file for you. **1** You have to extract it twice to get to the image file.

3 Windows 7 can burn disk images (IMG files) to CD or DVD, but not to USB. To do so, download Image Writer for Windows (http://bit.ly/imgwrite274). Point the software to the IMG file **1** and the USB device. **2**

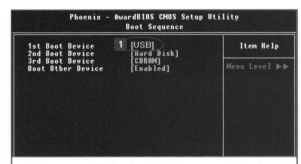

4 Restart your PC, leaving the USB memory drive plugged in. If your computer starts Windows, you'll need to restart again and enter your BIOS settings. Ensure USB is above your hard disk in the boot-priority order. **1**

5 Select your favoured language. English (United Kingdom) **1** is available from the More option. Choose the UK keyboard. **2** You need to connect to a network to sign in. A direct Ethernet connection **3** will be easiest, though it may also detect your Wi-Fi.

6 You can sign in with your Google Account, **1** choose Guest **2** if you'd prefer not to, or create a Google account **3** if you don't already have one. Choose an account picture and click OK.

7 The software launches straight into a browser. If you already sync your Chrome settings (from the spanner icon choose Options and Personal Stuff), your bookmarks and extensions will be there. **1**

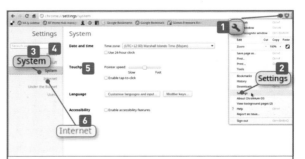

8 Click on the spanner icon **1** and choose Settings. **2** Click the System link **3** to control things like the system time **4** and pointer speed. **5** Networks can be managed from the Internet link. **6**

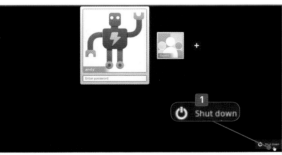

9 To shut down Chrome and return to Windows, click the spanner icon and select 'Sign out'. You'll return to the login screen. Choose to 'Shut down' **1** from there. To restart Windows, remove the USB memory drive and restart.

10 To run Chrome OS in Windows, download and extract the VirtualBox version from Step 1. Click New, **1** use the extracted file as the 'hard disk' and assign it up to 2GB of memory.

The Ultimate Guide to

Chapter 2
Google's best add-ons

Google Docs.............................. 19

Picasa... 21

iGoogle 22

Google Reader 23

One of the best things about Google is its enthusiasm for innovation. Unlike many other technology companies, the search giant has always been happy for third-party developers to take its products and do something new and interesting with them. Google even provides many of the resources required to customise its tools and has been known to incorporate outside ideas into its future releases. As a result, the internet is awash with tailored versions of Google's services and sites that can improve your web experience.

Over the next few pages, we reveal the best free Google 'upgrades' to enhance Google Docs, Picasa, iGoogle and Google Reader.

Google Docs

OffiSync
www.offisync.com

OffiSync is a useful tool that integrates Microsoft Office with Google Docs. You can save documents from the Desktop suite directly to Docs, and any changes you make online or off are automatically synced. The toolbar lets you find related content and information, and search the web and Google Images from within Office. The plug-in works with all versions of Office from 2003 upwards. See our Mini Workshop (right) to find out how to use OffiSync.

Open Document in Google Docs Viewer
http://bit.ly/open263

Install this Firefox add-on and, whenever you encounter an online document, you can just right-click the link and select

o 190	Open Link in New Tab
cestry.	Open Link in New Window
o 179	
o 180	Bookmark This Link
o 181	Save Link As...
o 182	Send Link...
o 183	Copy Link Location
o 184	Add to Picasa Web Albums
o 185	Adblock Plus: Block image...
o 186	

'Open Document in Google Docs' from the context menu (provided the originating site allows this). Open Document in Google Docs Viewer works with DOC, DOCX, PDF and PPT file types.

CloudMagic
www.cloudmagic.com

This browser add-on for Firefox and Chrome indexes your Google documents, Gmail inbox and contacts, to make finding a file, email or person significantly faster. It adds a search box to the right-hand side of Google Docs that

▶

MINI WORKSHOP | Connect Microsoft Office to Google Docs using OffiSync

1 Once you've installed OffiSync (www.offisync.com) and any necessary components, launch an Office program. You'll see a new OffiSync toolbar has been added just above the document window. Click the 'Open and Search for Files' yellow folder button. **1** You'll be prompted to log in with your Google Docs username and password. **2**

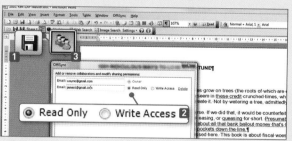

2 Once you're connected, you'll be able to open an existing document by clicking the Open button and browsing for the file you want. Save an Office document online by clicking the Save (disk) button. **1** You can choose who is able to access and edit the document. **2** The Merge (people) button **3** will blend changes from online collaborators.

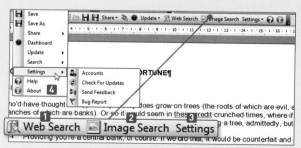

3 The toolbar lets you search the web from within Office **1** and browse for images to include in your documents. **2** The Settings button **3** lets you add, edit and remove Google accounts, and check for program updates. If you don't like having an extra toolbar, you can access the various OffiSync features from the main menu instead. **4**

displays and updates the results as you type. See our Mini Workshop (right) to find out how to use CloudMagic.

Insync
www.insynchq.com
Insync is similar to Dropbox (www.dropbox.com), but is aimed at Google Docs users. It lets you edit documents on

your Desktop, automatically saving the changes in the cloud as you make them. Sign in using your Google account and then just access your documents through the local Insync folder. The service is currently in private beta, but you can sign up for an invite.

Google Document List View
http://bit.ly/list263
This time-saving tool for Firefox adds a sidebar to the browser that lists all your Google Docs files. You can open documents by double-clicking them, and right-click a file to rename, hide or delete it.

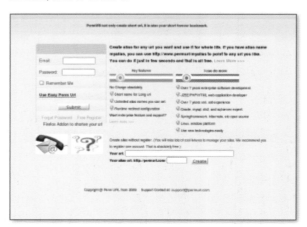

MINI WORKSHOP | Use CloudMagic to search your documents and emails

1 Install the relevant CloudMagic (www.cloudmagic.com) extension for Firefox or Chrome and then open Google Docs. You should see a new CloudMagic search box on the right-hand side of the interface. **1** Click the down arrow and select Manage Accounts, **2** then click the link to add a new account.

2 Enter the email address and password for the Google account you want to use. **1** You don't need to worry about security because the details are stored locally, rather than shared online. If you want to use CloudMagic with Gmail, you'll need to enable IMAP in Settings. Once done, the application will begin indexing your documents and messages.

3 Indexing may take some time to complete. Once it's done, you can use CloudMagic. Just type a document name, or some words from the body text, **1** and the tool will display matching results immediately. **2** You can preview a file's contents without leaving the current view, making it easy to copy and paste data between documents.

Picasa

Picasa Quick Viewer
http://bit.ly/picasa263

This Chrome add-on lets you view photos stored on Picasa Web Albums from wherever you are on the web. Click

the button and Picasa Quick Viewer will open a window of thumbnails. Click any image to view a larger version.

Live Writer Picasa Plugin
http://livewriterpicasa.codeplex.com

If you update your blog using Windows Live Writer this plug-in will let you to insert photos from Picasa Web Albums directly into your blog posts. Once installed, select Live Writer Picasa Plugin from the Insert menu, sign in with your Google Account and choose the photo you want.

AddToPicasa
http://bit.ly/addto263

Send any photos you find online directly to your Picasa Web Albums account using this simple Firefox add-on. Once

installed, right-click an image on the web and select the 'Add to Picasa Web Albums' option in the context menu.

Picasa Uploader for Facebook
http://apps.facebook.com/picasauploader

Install the Picasa Uploader and you'll be able to post images directly from Picasa to Facebook. Just select the photos

you want in the software, click the Facebook button at the bottom of the screen and click Start Upload.

FlashGrid Gallery
http://bit.ly/grid263

This Picasa template lets you display your photos in a full-screen Flash and XML-based gallery for the web. To use the

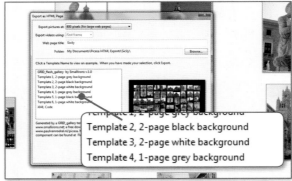

tool, extract its contents to a dedicated folder in C:\Program Files (x86)\Google\Picasa3\web\templates. Select the pictures you want in Picasa and then go to Folder, 'Export as HTML page' and select the template from the list.

iGoogle

Super iGoogle
http://geek-out-blog.blogspot.com

This add-on for Chrome or Firefox (with Greasemonkey installed) automatically removes the header, footer and sidebar tabs from iGoogle, making it neater and better suited for viewing on computers with small screens, such as netbooks. To choose what to display and what to hide, simply click the Settings button. You can also use the relevant keyboard shortcuts.

Wolfram Alpha
http://bit.ly/wolf263

Wolfram Alpha (below) focuses on providing answers to questions and calculations, and offers hundreds of useful iGoogle widgets covering a variety of subjects. You can view all the satellites over where you live, convert one unit of measurement into another, compare salaries for any profession in the world, and much more. Just select a widget, then click the iGoogle logo to embed it on your page.

Internet Bandwidth Test
http://bit.ly/speed263

If you want to know what your connection speed is at the beginning of each web session, add the Internet Bandwidth

Test widget to your iGoogle homepage. Just click the Start Bandwidth Test button for an instant speed check.

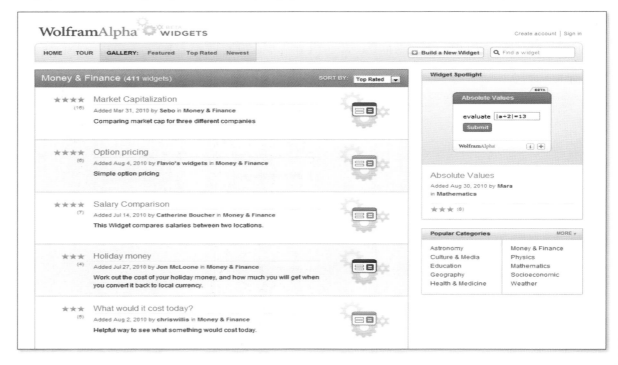

iGoogle Tab Remover
http://bit.ly/tab263
Although the main purpose of this Firefox add-on is to hide iGoogle's left navigation tabs to free up space, it also lets you reduce the size of the unnecessarily large top header.

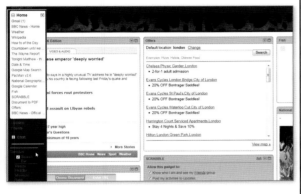

Hover your mouse over TimeDyn in the iGoogle Tabs menu, click Resize Header and then click anywhere in the header section to resize it to that point.

BBC News: Official UK Edition
www.bbc.co.uk/news/10628323
Catch up with the latest world and UK news by installing this free widget. The tabs let you view the top stories and video and audio clips. Click the More Stories link to open the full view. The links at the bottom will take you to the BBC home, news, sport and weather pages.

Google Reader

Google Reader Watcher
http://ajnasz.hu/google-reader-watcher
This Firefox add-on will periodically check Google Reader for unread feeds, and display the number of new stories next to the status and toolbar buttons. Hover your mouse over either of the icons to see how many unread stories

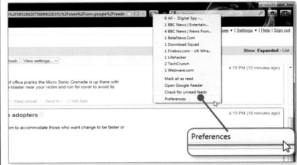

there are in the feed. The right-click menu lets you mark all the stories as read, open Google Reader, refresh the feed and customise the preferences.

Minimalist for Google Reader
http://bit.ly/min263
If you find Google Reader too cluttered, with lots of distracting features you never use, you can simplify it using

this Google Chrome add-on. Once installed, Minimalist for Google Reader lets you hide nearly 50 interface features, customise the colours, use a custom logo and more. Just tick the options you want in the menu, then load or refresh Reader to see the changes.

MagicCube FeedStore
http://bit.ly/magic263
Google Reader doesn't offer its own offline mode any more, but if you use Chrome you can still catch up on feeds when you're not connected to the internet by using this handy extension. MagicCube FeedStore monitors your account and caches a copy of any stories you receive, so you can read them later. Just click the button and the add-on will display the feeds in its own interface.

Better GReader
http://bit.ly/greader263
Better GReader is a brilliant add-on that lets you add a bunch of useful tools, including favicons, article previews and unread counts in your browser tab. It contains loads of attractive skins to customise Google Reader, making it look less drab and easier to use.

Google Reader Notifier for Windows
http://bit.ly/notifier263

This System Tray application alerts you when you have new unread items in Google Reader. Right-clicking the icon will let you set preferences, such as how often to check for new feeds. You can have the program play an audio notification file, and also set it to alert you only when items tagged with specific keywords appear.

FeedSquares
http://bit.ly/feed263
This Chrome add-on displays Google Reader feeds in a tiled wall (below). You can see at a glance how many unread stories a feed has, and also view top picks and shared stories from your friends.

If there are any photos in a post, FeedSquares will show image previews. Click a feed to view the stories in a strip at the bottom of the screen.

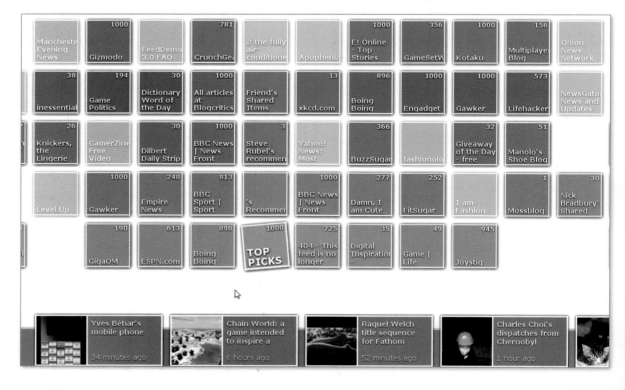

OUR MASSIVE

End of summer sale is here!

With huge discounts on some of our most exciting products

Save up to **80%**

Get 3 months **FREE**

Get 3 months **FREE**

Save up to **25%**

Domain names
Now is the time to register your ideal domain with huge savings on .me, .co and .info domains.

Unlimited hosting
Everything you need to create your perfect website with unlimited features.

SiteFusion
Use our flexible site builder to build a professional website without any coding knowledge.

SSL certificates
There is no better time to protect your users and secure all sensitive data.

You can see all our BIG discounts online right now at **123-reg.co.uk/sale**

But hurry – our BIG sale is for a limited time only!

Start saving now at 123-reg.co.uk/sale

The Ultimate Guide to
Google's Hidden Tools

Chapter 3
Secret search tips

**Google's improved
search features** 28

**Smarter and faster
Google searches** 30

Remove junk search results 32

**Advanced tips for
Google Desktop Search** 33

Google's improved search features

Google is always improving its search features to make it easier and faster to find what you want. Here are nine of the latest changes

See all search results on one page

Google is bringing infinite scrolling to its search results, which will mean you'll no longer having to click through pages of links and wait for them to load separately. As you scroll down through the results, you will soon be able to click a 'Show more results' bar at the bottom of the page and the next list of links appears underneath, instead of on a separate page.

Listen to music within your search results

Now, when you search for artists or tracks in Google.com, you can access snippets of music within the search results. If any of the listed sites contain video or audio content a list of this will appear under the website link. Videos are denoted by a small play button, while music is shown using musical notes. If the link needs to redirect you to another site, you will be asked if you want to be sent there or returned to the search results. At the moment, it's only available in the UK when you search using Google.com.

Share results using +1

You can now recommend sites you like to your friends using the +1 button. Up until Google+ launched, the +1 button was akin to Facebook's Like button, in that all it did was show that you're interested in a link. Now with Google+, you can share these sites with your Circles. Click the +1 button next to a link, and it will grab an image and a snippet of the text from the page. You can then choose to share it with select Circles. You can access your +1 sites through your Google profile at all times, and share it later if you want too.

Get related content quicker

Using a specially designed toolbar – in Internet Explorer and Firefox – or a dedicated Chrome extension, you can now get access to related content within your browser while searching using Google. For example, if you search for a restaurant, once you click the result the Google Related toolbar at the bottom of the page will appear to show a map of the area, related reviews and web pages, images and alternative restaurants. You don't have to click away from the page you're on either; you can click the tabs on the Toolbar and they will appear in a small window. Even videos can be played direct from the Toolbar.

Jump to website sections with improved Site Links

Site Links aren't new to Google search results, but up until recently they were shown in a small list of links below

the main site result. Google has improved these links, expanding them to show the individual URL of each as well as a small text preview of what the page contains. The amount of links has increased from eight to 12, where applicable, too.

Get search results from Google+ posts

Social Search was launched back in 2009 to show your friends' relevant Twitter and Facebook posts within search results. So it makes sense that since Google has launched its own social network, Google+ posts are included, too. To get this feature, you have to be signed into your Google

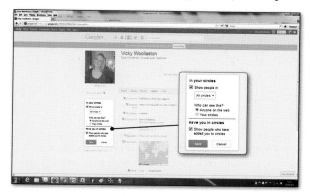

account as it will only show posts made by people you're connected with. It will also only show posts that have been shared 'Publically'. From your Google+ news feed, you can see which posts are public. If you don't want your results to show up in other people's searches, set your posts to Private by clicking the gear icon in the top-right of your profile. Choose Google+ Settings, then Profile and Privacy.

Search by voice or picture

Voice and picture search is now available on desktops after being introduced to mobiles in 2008 and 2009 respectively.

To use Google Voice you need a working microphone on your PC. To activate it, click the microphone icon on the search box and speak your query.

Google Goggles is the picture search app for mobiles, but if you have a picture of something you want to look for you can now upload it into the search engine on your PC. Go to http://images.google.com and drag an image into the search box.

Alternatively, paste the URL of the image or upload it from your hard drive by clicking the camera to the right of the search box.

Jump directly to relevant bits of search results

One annoying feature of Google is that after searching for a particular phrase, when you click the link you then have to hunt through the text to find exactly where your query is. The Chrome Google Quick Scroll extension solves this problem. Once installed, every time you make a specific search and click the link a small pop-up box appears in the bottom right-hand corner, with links to the parts of the text that are most relevant. It highlights the text in yellow, too.

The feature also integrates in Instant previews so before you click a result, hover your mouse over to get the preview. The most relevant text will then be highlighted on the preview.

Test out Google's latest search features

Google may have done away with its Labs site, but it still has a couple of testing platforms for different products. You can join its search feature experiments at www.google.com/experimental and test them out before they are released. Current experiments include Google's Instant search feature being developed for images and search keyboard shortcuts. You can also keep up to date with all changes in Google search at http://insidesearch.blogspot.com.

Smarter and faster Google searches

There are lots of ingenious ways to improve your Google searches. Here are eight of our favourites

TOP SEARCH TIPS

Control Google Instant with your keyboard
Google Instant displays search results as you type, saving you time, but you can make it work even faster by using keyboard shortcuts instead of your mouse. Type in part or all of a word, then use the up and down arrow keys on your keyboard to move through the suggested search terms and view the results. Hit Enter to confirm your search. You can now use the up and down keys to move through the results of the search. Hit Enter again to open the website of your choice.

Find nearby places of interest
Places is a search feature that allows you to discover businesses, restaurants and other services in a particular area. Go to Google Search and enter the type of thing you're looking for, along with a location – 'fish and chips in Warrington' (without the quotes), for example – and Google will present you with a list of possible choices. If

you leave the location blank, Places will use your current position for the search area.

Preview sites without clicking
If you want to see what a website looks like before you visit it, click the 'More search tools' option and select 'Page previews'. A thumbnail will appear next to the various search results. You can turn this feature off at any time by clicking the X in the 'Page previews' banner above the results. Curiously, this option seems to appear only intermittently in Chrome.

View translated pages
If you limit yourself to viewing only English language pages in searches, you might miss some important results. To see related foreign-language sites helpfully translated by Google, click the 'More search tools' option on the left-hand side of the search results and select 'Translated foreign pages'. You can add and remove languages as required.

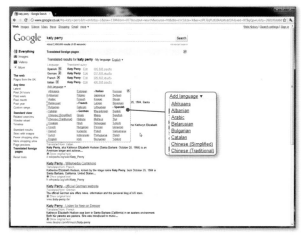

SECRET SEARCH TIPS

BEST SEARCH ADD-ONS

Surf Canyon
www.surfcanyon.com/extension.jsp

The aim of this browser add-on is to make Google's search results more relevant to you. To view real-time recommendations based on your activity, click the bull's-eye target next to any result and Surf Canyon's personalisation feature will suggest pages you might

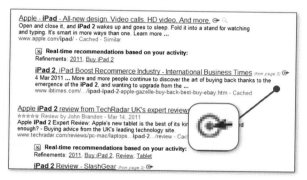

otherwise have missed. The add-on works with Internet Explorer, Firefox and Chrome and can also be used for Yahoo and Bing searches.

Google Cache Continue Redux
http://bit.ly/redux263

Google always makes a copy of web pages as it indexes them. This means that if the site you're searching for has gone down, or has been removed for any reason, you'll be able to view individual pages from this cache. If you want to browse the entire site (or as much of it as has been saved) you'll need this clever user script. For Chrome and Opera, get it by clicking the Install button on the web page.

For Firefox, you'll first need to install the Greasemonkey extension (http://bit.ly/cache263).

SearchPreview
http://searchpreview.de

Formerly known as GooglePreview, this Firefox add-on inserts thumbnail images of websites next to Google search results (and Yahoo and Bing, too). You can turn the feature

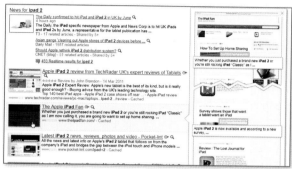

on or off at any time by clicking the SearchPreview icon in your browser's status bar.

StartingPage
http://startingpage.com

Most search engines, including Google, store information about you such as your IP address, search terms you've used and links you've followed. StartingPage helps to protect your privacy by continuing to deliver the results you want without spying on you. The site is powered by Google, so you'll get exactly the same results, but it won't record your IP address, use tracking cookies or share any information with third parties.

Remove junk search results

Google has faced criticism for the amount of spam in its search results. We reveal 10 ways to clean up your searches

Filter spam using SafeSearch

Turning on SafeSearch eliminates explicit sexual content from Google's search results. To activate this feature, go to Google Preferences (www.google.com/preferences), scroll to SafeSearch Filtering and choose 'Use strict filtering'.

Scan your results for malware

McAfee SiteAdvisor (www.siteadvisor.com) and AVG LinkScanner (http://linkscanner.avg.com) scan your search results and display a green tick next to pages that are safe to visit and a red cross by dangerous sites that contain malware and other threats.

Filter spam in Firefox

If you have the Greasemonkey (www.greasespot.net) extension installed in Firefox, you can use a script called Noise Reduction for Google & Bing (http://bit.ly/noise260) to strip spam from search results. Click the Filter button next to a bad page to remove it from future results. Note that the script won't work while Google Instant is running.

Block spam in Chrome

If you use Chrome, the extension Search Filter (http://bit.ly/search260) does a similar job to Noise Reduction. Just click the red 'no entry' icon below a dodgy search result to block that page in future. Again, the add-on won't work properly if Google Instant is turned on.

Report spam to Google

You can help Google improve its search results by reporting any spam sites you encounter. Go to the 'Spam report' page (http://bit.ly/spam260), type in the web address of the site that is 'misbehaving' and the search query that took you there. Specify the type of problem you encountered – for example, misleading words – and click 'Report spam'.

Exclude keywords from searches

To stop your searches producing irrelevant results, you can exclude specific terms and websites using a '-' sign. For example, to find pages about opera but not the Opera web browser, you could type 'opera –browser'.

Remove ads from search results

You can also remove adverts from search results using the Firefox add-on OptimizeGoogle (www.optimizegoogle.com). Go into Options, click Web in the left-hand column and tick the option 'Remove ads'. Click Filter and you can choose to block specific domains from your results.

Turn searches into RSS feeds

If you often look up the same search terms, use Google Alerts (www.google.com/alerts) to deliver results you've not already seen in the form of a clean RSS feed. Enter your search terms, choose the type of results and select Feed from the 'Deliver to:' menu. Click Create Alert and, on the next page, click the Feed link to get the RSS address.

Include 'solved' in searches

If you've got a problem with your PC, try including the word 'solved' in your searches. This will take you to technical-discussion forums where a similar query was satisfactorily answered and marked as 'solved', rather than wasting your time with results that just ask the same thing.

Create a Custom Search Engine

Google Custom Search (www.google.co.uk/cse) is a free service that lets you create a personalised search engine that searches only the sites you specify. It also serves as an effective means of keeping your results free of spam. You can include as many pages, sites and domains as you want and name your search engine whatever you like.

Advanced tips for Google Desktop Search

Did you know you can use Google Desktop Search as a program launcher and sync its sidebar tools across multiple computers? We show you how

1 Google Desktop Search will automatically index a number of key locations on your hard disk to make it easier to search for files. Click within the Search box found in the sidebar, **1** type the name of a program **2** and click its entry in the list to launch the application. **3**

2 To make it easier to use Google Desktop Search as a program launcher, press Ctrl twice in quick succession to display the Search window, **1** then click the Options link. **2** Tick the box labelled Launch Programmes/Files **3** and click Close **4** before performing a search.

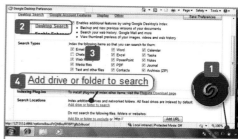

3 By default, Google Desktop Search will index certain key locations and file types. To include more, right-click the System Tray icon, **1** select Options, go to Desktop Search **2** and tick the boxes relating to items you'd like to index. **3** Click the link in Search Locations to add extra folders. **4**

4 As well as being used to index and search your local files, the software can be used to search your Gmail Inbox. Right-click the System Tray icon, **1** select Options and go to Google Account Features. **2** Tick the box, **3** enter your account details and click Save Preferences. **4**

5 Google Desktop Search's extendibility is particularly impressive. Right-click an empty section of the sidebar and select 'Add gadgets'. **1** Use the category link to the left **2** to browse through the available gadgets. Click the Add button beneath a gadget's icon to install the tool.

6 If you regularly work with more than one computer, you can sync Google Desktop Search gadgets between them. Right-click an empty section of the sidebar, select 'Configure gadgets' and tick the box at the top. **1** Enter your Google address and password, **2** then click OK and OK again. **3**

The Ultimate Guide to
Google's Hidden Tools

Chapter 4

Get more from Chrome

Best new Chrome add-ons 36

**Install and manage
Chrome extensions** 40

Tighten up Chrome's security 41

Best new Google Chrome add-ons

Chrome is now more popular than Firefox, and there are lots of ways to make it even better. Here are 21 of the most useful new add-ons

Listen to music as you browse the web
http://bit.ly/music274
Music+ is an excellent new Chrome extension that lets you listen to and share songs by your favourite artists as you browse the web. Simply search for an act to view available tracks and then click to play them. The add-on continues to work in the background as you go about your online activities

and lets you queue songs by additional artists to listen to later. Music+ also features Facebook integration for sharing streams with your friends.

Capture screen grabs of websites
http://bit.ly/capture274
Awesome Screenshot: Capture & Annotate is a simple but useful Chrome add-on that makes it incredibly easy to take screen grabs of websites.

The latest version of the extension lets you choose to capture whole pages or just the area visible in your browser, annotate and highlight sections of the image, and save the grab to your hard disk as a PNG file. You can also share the screenshot online using the popular free bookmarking tool Diigo (www.diigo.com).

Prevent websites distracting you
http://bit.ly/stay274
If you often find yourself checking Facebook and browsing Amazon when you should be working, this extension can boost your productivity. StayFocusd lets you block time-wasting websites, so you can concentrate on the job at hand. To stop access being forbidden altogether, you can set a maximum number of minutes per day that you'll be allowed to browse blocked sites. Just click the toolbar button to block or allow specific pages and sites.

Always bring new tabs to the front
http://bit.ly/tabs274
When you right-click a URL in Chrome and choose 'Open link in new tab', the page always opens in the background behind your current tabs. Install Tabs to the Front, however, and new tabs will open in the foreground by default, so you can view their content immediately.

Add Facebook events to Google Calendar
http://bit.ly/facebook274
If you organise your life using Google Calendar, this handy extension lets you add Facebook events such as birthdays to your calendar in a couple of clicks. This saves you having

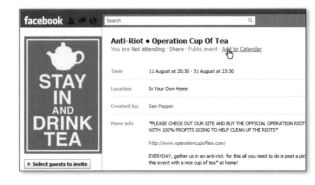

to enter or copy and paste the details manually. Once you've installed the Add Facebook Events extension, an 'Add to Calendar' option will appear at the top of Facebook event pages. Click this and then click Save to add the event to your Google Calendar.

Look up definitions on web pages
http://bit.ly/dictionary274

If you come across a word on a web page that you don't recognise or understand, you can use the official Google Dictionary extension to find out what it means. Just double-click the word to view a definition in a pop-up bubble, or click the toolbar button, enter a word and click Define. Foreign words are automatically translated into English and the latest version of the extension lets you click a speaker icon to hear a word's correct pronunciation.

Filter content about annoying people
http://bit.ly/silence274

Are you tired of reading stories about David Beckham or Cheryl Cole every time you visit your favourite news website? If so, why not 'gag' them using the Chrome extension Silence of the Celebs. This filters articles about ubiquitous people on sites including Google News, Twitter and CNN. You can 'silence' any person or word you want, and remove entries such as Tom Cruise and Lady Gaga from the extension's default list.

Share content on social networks
http://bit.ly/sync274

Recognising that many of us now have accounts with Facebook, Twitter and Google+, this extension lets you post links, messages and photos to all three social networks simultaneously. Publish Sync for Google+ & Facebook (Green Edition) also lets you share content from one site on a rival

service and, in the case of Google+, choose which circles it will appear in. You can easily log out of an account to prevent your posts being synchronised.

Find and mute noisy browser tabs
www.mutetab.com

One of the problems with having lots of browser tabs open is that if one starts making a noise, such as playing a video advert or loading a game, it can take a lot of clicking to find the culprit. MuteTab solves this problem by showing you a list

Tabs that are possibly making sound

Current tab
The 'Life of Brian' Debate (1979) - YouTube
http://www.youtube.com/watch?v=TqAHHhr7vmU&feature=feedrec_grec_index
Show Mute (Unsafe) Mute (Safe) Restore Close

All tabs
Mute (Unsafe) Mute (Safe) Restore Close

All other tabs
Mute (Unsafe) Mute (Safe) Restore Close

Other individual tabs (most recent first)
(none)

of tabs that are potentially making a sound, and letting you silence or close them with a single click.

Keep your family safe online
http://bit.ly/webfilter274

WebFilter helps to protect your children from pornographic, violent and other unsuitable web content, as well as sites that host spyware, spam and phishing scams. Once installed, simply go to Tools, Extensions, Options and choose the categories you want to block. Any attempt to visit a forbidden site will result in a 'Web Access Blocked' message. WebFilter works well for a free tool but savvy kids may soon learn how to disable it.

Share all your open tabs in one link
http://bit.ly/tabulate274

Tabulate provides a useful means of saving all the websites you currently have open in Chrome as a single, shortened

URL. This makes it easy to share multiple tabs via email or on social networks. To create the aggregated link, click the 'Grab your tabs!' button on the toolbar. The URL, which always begins with 'http://bridgeurl.com' is copied to your clipboard automatically so you can paste it into a program or website.

Change the appearance of web pages
http://bit.ly/style274

Stylebot lets you adjust the way websites look and feel by playing around with custom style sheets (CSS). Usually, this involves some knowledge of web design but the extension makes it easy for anyone to change the fonts, colours and layout of different page elements. Stylebot saves your alterations, which gives you free rein to customise your favourite sites to suit your tastes. It also offers advanced tools for inspecting and editing CSS.

Conceal comments in Google+
http://bit.ly/gme274

One complaint about Google+ is that all the comments on a post are displayed at once, unlike Facebook, which only shows the most recent two. These can take up valuable screen space,

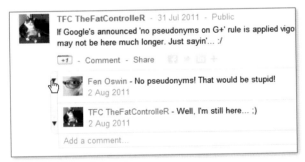

especially if people in your circles attract lots of comments. Help is at hand in the form of G+me for Google Plus, which lets you 'collapse' comments to keep them hidden until you want to expand and read them. You can also collapse a particular person's posts.

Block junk sites from search results
http://bit.ly/personal274

Earlier this year, Google released Personal Blocklist for Chrome, which stops 'content farms' – websites containing low-quality content – appearing in search results. The extension has now been updated to make it even more effective at blocking junk sites. You can import lists of 'patterns' that will automatically filter results similar to sites

you choose to block, and block the host as well as the domain of the currently active tab.

Find the cheapest products and flights
www.getinvisiblehand.com

The latest version of price-comparison tool InvisibleHand saves you money on air travel. When you're looking for cheap flights online, the extension will tell you where you can get the

best deal and let you click through to the relevant site to book. You can use the tool to compare the cost of hotels, rental cars and thousands of products. InvisibleHand is also available for Firefox and Internet Explorer.

Access Picasa Web Albums from Chrome
http://bit.ly/picasa274

Picasa Extension is a simple but very useful Chrome add-on that gives you instant access to Google's photo-sharing service Picasa Web Albums. Click the Picasa logo on your browser's toolbar to view thumbnail images of all your albums, and then click one to open it. You can also read comments that have been posted on your photos.

Add Google +1 to all web pages
http://bit.ly/plus274

Google's new +1 feature, which lets you share web content you like with your friends and contacts, has already been added to thousands of sites. But there are still plenty that

don't yet offer a +1 option, which is where this add-on comes in. The '+1 Button – Plus One Button' extension lets you add your stamp of approval to any web page with a single click. You can also see at a glance how many other people have shared the same content.

Get rain alerts in your browser
http://bit.ly/rain274

Be prepared for the next downpour by installing Rain Alarm, which displays an alert when precipitation is heading your way. This weather add-on automatically detects where you are and if you click the toolbar button, you can view a Google Maps mash-up forecasting the movement and heaviness of rain across the UK over the next 24 hours. Rain Alarm also features Desktop notifications that will keep you informed when Chrome is closed.

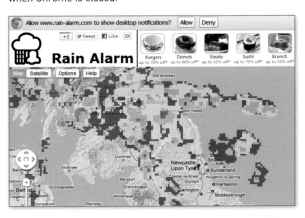

Hide selected Facebook friends
http://bit.ly/hide274

Although Facebook lets you 'hide' people in your News Feed, they can still pop up in other sections of the site, such as photo albums and profile updates. If you want to hear less from a particular person without de-friending them, install the Chrome extension Eternal Sunshine. This lets you conceal content from uninteresting Facebook acquaintances, without having to reduce your friend count. You can easily 'unhide' them if you change your mind.

Turn any site into a game of Asteroids
http://bit.ly/asteroids274

Blast boring websites to bits with the aid of Kick Ass, a fun Chrome add-on that lets you transform any website into an Asteroids-type game. Once activated, you can move your triangular spaceship around the page using the cursor keys

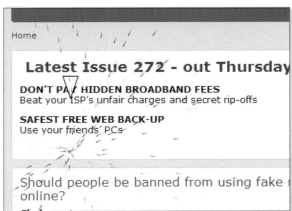

and press the Spacebar to destroy individual elements. Cleverly, you can use Kick Ass to strip away parts of a page prior to printing, so it has a practical purpose as well as a time-wasting one.

Edit web pages and photos using Picnik
http://bit.ly/picnik274

The Chrome extension for the Google-owned online image editor Picnik (www.picnik.com) lets you capture and edit photos and pages you come across while browsing the web. Just click the toolbar button and either choose 'Send the visible page to Picnik' or select a specific image. The copied content will open in Picnik where you can resize, crop and rotate it, adjust the colours and exposure, and apply a range of effects before saving and sharing the result.

Install and manage Chrome extensions

Make Chrome work smoother by installing and organising add-ons

1 To add extensions to Chrome, go to the Extensions Gallery (https://chrome.google.com/extensions). Here you can browse the add-ons on offer by clicking the 'Most popular', 'Most recent' and 'Top rated' links on the left **1** or find a specific extension using the search box. **2** There are also Featured extensions, **3** as chosen by Google, that are updated every day.

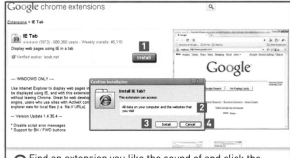

2 Find an extension you like the sound of and click the blue Install button **1** on its description page. A Confirm Installation box will appear that tells you exactly what information on your computer the extension will be able to access – for example, your data on all websites. **2** If you're happy with this, click the Install button **3** to continue; if not, click Cancel. **4**

3 Once the extension has been installed, a dedicated button may appear on your Chrome toolbar. Usually, you can right-click this and select Options to adjust the extension's settings. If no toolbar button has appeared, you can access the options for the extension by clicking the Settings (spanner) button **1** and going to Tools, **2** Extensions. **3**

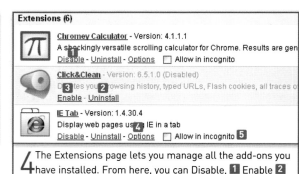

4 The Extensions page lets you manage all the add-ons you have installed. From here, you can Disable, **1** Enable **2** and Uninstall **3** an extension, and open its Options. **4** You can also choose to let the add-on run in Chrome's private-browsing mode by choosing 'Allow in incognito'. **5** Click 'Get more extensions' to return to the Extensions Gallery.

Tighten up Chrome's security

We look at ways to tighten up Google Chrome's built-in security settings and show you how to install and use security-boosting extensions

1 Google Chrome can save passwords on any site you visit, but they're easy to view so it's a serious security problem if you share your PC with others. To disable this function, click the Spanner icon **1** and choose Options. Under the Personal Stuff tab, **2** select 'Never save passwords' **3** and Close. **4**

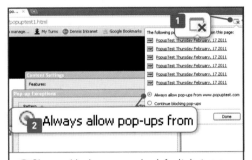

2 Chrome blocks pop-ups by default, but you can let them display on some sites. Click the icon in the address bar **1** and select 'Always allow pop-ups from'. **2** To remove the site later, go back to Options and select the 'Under the hood' tab. Choose 'Content settings', Pop-ups and Exceptions.

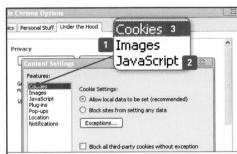

3 Disabling images **1** completely is a bit over the top, but you might want to block JavaScript and cookies by default, letting trusted sites through as you go. Go to 'Content settings' to block JavaScript **2** and cookies. **3** Trusted sites can be added in the same way as Step 2.

4 The McAfee Site Advisor extension (http://bit.ly/mcafee261) scans sites for potential threats and checks for adware in downloads. A tick icon **1** denotes a safe site, a cross means a threat is detected. You can manage options and notifications through Tools, **2** Extensions. **3**

5 The KidSafe LinkExtend extension (http://bit.ly/kidsafe261) blocks unsuitable content. It gives ratings for child safety on each site – click the icon **1** to display them. A warning appears if a site contains adult content and you can then block it. Other options are managed in Tools.

6 Use the Personal Blocklist extension (http://bit.ly/blocklist261) to block certain domains or hosts in Google searches. Once it's installed, click the Block link **1** under a result to block it in future searches. To unblock or edit sites you've blocked, click the hand icon **2** next to the address bar.

The Ultimate Guide to
Google's Hidden Tools

Chapter 5

Google Earth and Maps

Best Google Maps for holidays....... 44

12 secrets for Google Street View.. 46

**Geolocate your photos
in Google Earth from Picasa** 48

Customise a Google Map 49

**Combine Ordnance
Survey maps with Google** 50

**Create your own
Google Earth video** 52

Best Google Maps for holidays

We reveal 14 great Google Maps tools that will help you plan every aspect of your holiday, while saving you time, hassle and money

Check your train is running

If you're wondering if your train is going to arrive on time or if it's been delayed several counties away, have a look

at Accessible UK Train Timetables' live map (http://traintimes.org.uk/map). This lets you view all trains approaching 25 mainline stations across the UK – from Aberdeen to Southampton Central – in real time. The yellow pins represent stations and the red ones are trains.

Save money on air travel

You can track down bargain flights using Skyscanner's 'Cheap flight route' map (www.skyscanner.net/cheap-

flights-map). Enter a departure airport, choose where you want to go (or leave it blank if you just want to find out what's available) and enter the dates you wish to travel and the number of passengers. Skyscanner will then show you the cheapest airlines. You can also search for hotels and car hire.

Get an instant travel guide

Travel-information site Tixik (http://en.tixik.com) offers thousands of useful guides for locations all over the world. Just select a city or sight, and Tixik will tell you about it, display a map and some photos, and let you find accommodation, book flights, rent a vehicle and more. You even get a seven-day weather forecast for that location.

Find and book cheap hotels

Google Maps has now added hotel prices to its built-in data options. Search for a hotel to see an approximate price per night, then click the price box to view the rate from various websites including Expedia, Hotels.com and Booking.com. To check availability and book a room, click the name of the hotel.

View hotels before you book

If you're picky about where you stay, you can use Expedia's Hotel View (www.expediahotelview.co.uk) to see exactly what your potential choice of accommodation looks like, and explore the surrounding area. Enter a landmark or location,

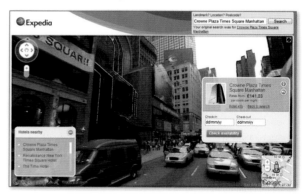

or search for a hotel by name, then click the View Hotel button to see the results in Street View. Expedia will also show you any nearby alternative accommodation, and let you check room availability.

Avoid political protests and strikes

The Middle East is obviously a hotspot for political upheaval at the moment, but there are plenty of other places you should think twice about visiting. Check out Unleashed

Tactical's Civil Unrest Map (http://bit.ly/unrest271) and *The Guardian*'s FCO Travel Advice Map (http://bit.ly/guardian271) to see the countries and regions to avoid.

Get taxi fare prices

World Taximeter (www.worldtaximeter.com) is a useful site that gives you a rough idea of how much a journey will cost before you jump in the back of a cab. Pick your city

(the site currently covers 39 locations, including the UK, US and many European cities) and tell World Taximeter where you want to leave from, your destination, and the time that you'll be travelling. The prices on the resulting map should only ever be treated as rough estimates, but at least you'll have a ballpark figure of what you should be paying.

Predict the weather based on past trends

It's always useful to know what the weather is going to be like before you pack your case. WeatherSpark (www.weatherspark.com) displays the current conditions and a future forecast for any UK or global destination, and also lets you view detailed historical information about past weather. This lets you see, for example, if your destination often experiences snow in September.

Discover the nearest Wi-Fi hotspots

When you're out and about in a foreign country or strolling around the rural beauty spots of the UK, finding Wi-Fi hotspots away from an airport or hotel can be difficult. JiWire's directory (http://bit.ly/jiwire271) tells you the location of more than 560,000 free and paid-for wireless-access points across 142 countries. Just choose your location and browse the list or explore the map to find the hotspots nearest to you.

Plan bus journeys in London

London has an extensive bus network, but it can be confusing if you're not familiar with it. Fortunately, BusIt London (www.busitlondon.co.uk) can help. Enter your start and end points to view all the available routes on the map. The site will tell you where to get on and off, and what bus number you need.

Find the nearest cash machine

If you find yourself stuck in a strange city without any money, you can use the Mastercard ATM locator (www.mastercard.co.uk/atm-locator.html) to find the nearest cash machine. Select your current country or region, enter an address, town or postal code and add a search radius.

Find the quickest and cheapest route

Whether you're planning to travel by plane, train or automobile, Rome2rio (www.rome2rio.com) will display the easiest travel routes and tell you the cheapest prices, as well as approximate travel times. Type your departure and destination points to get the best route, along with five alternatives.

Use live information to avoid traffic jams

If you're going on a long journey, the last thing you want is to be stuck in a traffic jam. Route Scanner (www.routescanner.co.uk) displays live traffic information to help you avoid any blackspots, accidents and tailbacks along the way. Google Maps' built-in Traffic layer can also show you the speed of moving traffic.

Create your own Google Map mash-up

If you want to share details of your trip with friends, try creating an animated map using Animaps (www.animaps.com). This free tool lets you customise a Google Map by adding moving markers that display images, videos and text at the appropriate points. The Animap takes the form of a video, which you can share by email or upload to YouTube and Facebook. Note that Animaps won't work in versions of Internet Explorer earlier than IE9.

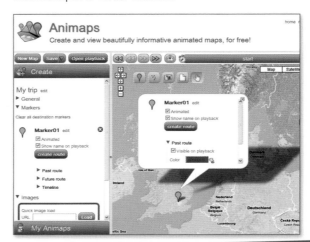

12 secrets for Google Street View

Street View is full of surprises and useful hidden tools. We reveal 12 ways to get more from Google's amazing service

Turn the pegman into a skier or a penguin

The yellow 'pegman' icon, which brings up Street View imagery when you drag it onto a location, has a couple of interesting variations. Go to Blackcomb Mountain in Vancouver (http://bit.ly/pegmanski265), for example, and the pegman gains a skiing outfit and a pair of skis. And when you explore the Street View imagery for Half Moon Island, Antarctica (http://bit.ly/pegpen265), the pegman is transformed into a penguin, which you can move around.

Take the pegman on a world tour

The Street View website (http://maps.google.com/streetview) features a global map that shows you where imagery is available internationally. To access it, click the Learn menu at the top of the page and choose 'Where is Street View?'. Next, drag the pegman to different countries around the world to get a close-up look at the US, Australia, South Africa, part of Brazil and many parts of Europe.

View driving directions in Street View

If you use the Get Directions feature in Google Maps (http://maps.google.co.uk) to guide you from A to B, you can trace your route visually in Street View. Enter where you're

travelling from and to, as usual, and click Get Directions. Scroll down to the turn-by-turn instructions, hover your mouse over an individual step and the pegman icon will appear. Click it to see the location in Street View on the right, and then move the pegman along the blue line to continue your journey.

Explore Street View in 3D

When Google added a 3D mode to Street View on 1 April 2010, most of us assumed it was an April Fools' joke, although the 3D pegman remained available for a while afterwards. What few realise is that you can still access the 3D mode – just press QWERTY on your keyboard to activate 3D. You will, of course, need 3D glasses with red- and green lenses to get the full effect.

Add Street View imagery to your website

Street View lets you add a 360° panorama of one of your favourite places to your website or blog. Open the location you want to share, click the Link button above the main window and click 'Customize or preview embedded map'. Choose whether to use a small, medium or large version of the panorama, or enter the exact width and height of your

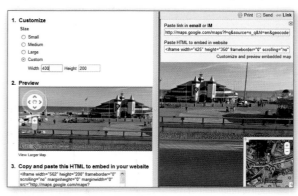

choice, and copy the HTML provided into the code of your website or blog. Visitors will be able to zoom in and out, and move around the Street View imagery in the usual way.

Navigate Street View using your keyboard

You can explore Street View imagery using your keyboard. Press the A and D keys to rotate your view left and right, and use W and S to tilt up and down. Alternatively, you can just use the arrow keys. You'll need to click on the main image first in order to use keyboard shortcuts.

Use Street View on your smartphone

The Google Maps apps for Android, BlackBerry and iPhone (www.google.com/mobile/maps) all now include Street View imagery. Just search for an address as usual, tap it to view the details and then press the pegman option to load Street View. You can use the Compass Mode, which tells you which direction you're looking in, to help you get your bearings.

Use Street View in Google Earth

If you prefer to browse the world using Google Earth (http://earth.google.co.uk) rather than Google Maps, you can still get all the benefits of Street View imagery. The latest version of the virtual globe, Google Earth 6, integrates Street View – just drag the pegman onto an area to zoom down and explore it as if you were really there. You can use the building icon in the top-right corner to switch between Street View and Google Earth's ground-level view.

Grab paintings from famous art galleries

Google's Street View-powered Art Project (www. googleartproject.com) has an interesting feature that lets you create a virtual art collection of your favourite paintings. When you're exploring a gallery and see a piece

you like, click the 'Create an Artwork Collection' button in the bottom-right corner. Click 'Add artwork view to your collection', zoom and pan the picture to capture a specific part or the whole thing, and click the Save View button.

Access Street View from property websites

If you're looking to buy or rent a house and want to know the type of area you're moving into, install the Chrome extension PropertyWizza UK (http://bit.ly/property265). This gives you access to property information, including Street View, when you're browsing Rightmove (www.rightmove. co.uk) and Zoopla (www.zoopla.co.uk). When data for a particular address is available, the toolbar button lights up. Click it and choose Dual Maps from the drop-down menu to see imagery from Google and Bing, with Street View in the top left. PropertyWizza UK also provides details of house prices, planning applications and flood risk.

Explore the area around a hotel

If you're planning to book a swanky hotel, make sure it's not situated next to a busy road using Expedia Hotel View (www. expediahotel.co.uk). This service uses Street View to show you the areas immediately surrounding hotels in London, New York, Madrid and many other cities. If you like what you see, you can specify your preferred dates and click through to Expedia (www.expedia.co.uk) in order to book your room.

Explore historic sites and landmarks

Save money on a sightseeing holiday by checking out some of the wonders of the world via Street View. The new Gallery section of the website (http://bit.ly/gallery265) lets you explore areas and landmarks around the world. These include the Colosseum in Rome, Niagara Falls, the Eiffel Tower and Stonehenge.

Geolocate your photos in Google Earth from Picasa

Geolocating your photos adds a new dimension to viewing and sharing them. Once they have a location added to them, you can even view them in Google Earth

1 Open Picasa (http://picasa.google.com) and choose the photos folder or album **1** you want to assign a particular location to. Click the Places button **2** to open the Places sidebar. **3** Search for a location, **4** or change the map type **5** and scroll around it to pinpoint the exact location.

2 Click the green map marker button **1** and click again where you want the photos to be located. You can drag the marker around the map to get it to the right spot. When you're happy, click OK **2** in the 'Place photos here' box. Repeat for all the photos you want to locate.

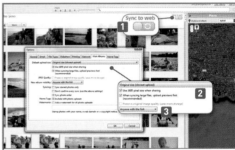

3 Make sure all your geolocated photos are selected and flick the 'Sync to web' switch. **1** You'll need to sign into your Google account, if you haven't already. Click Change Settings to choose your upload options, such as size **2** and privacy settings. **3** When you're done, simply click Sync.

4 Go to your Picasa Web Albums page (http://picasaweb.google.com) and click the album you just uploaded. You should see your photos and a map of their location. **1** Click an individual photo to fine-tune its placement. Under the map, click 'Edit location' **2** and move the marker on the map. **3**

5 You can also 'Upload to Panoramio' if you'd like your pictures to appear when people browse the area on Google Earth (http://earth.google.co.uk). Return to the Album view and click the 'View in Google Earth' link. **1** Save the file it links to somewhere safe. **2**

6 From Google Earth's File menu, **1** choose Open and load the file. The map will zoom to a view that covers all your photos. To turn everyone else's photos off, untick Photos under Layers. **2** Your photos are listed in Temporary Places. **3** To make them permanent, drag them into My Places. **4**

Customise a Google Map

When you're trying to find your way around, nothing beats local knowledge. We show you how to use Google Maps to make sure that everyone is kept in the loop

1 In Google Maps (http://maps.google.co.uk) enter your Gmail username and password and click 'My places' **1**, followed by the create new map button. **2** Enter a title and description and decide if you want it to be public, which means anyone can find it by searching, or Unlisted, so only those with the link can see it.

2 Zoom into the map to see available locations; use the search bar if necessary. Once you've found something you want to highlight, click its name on the map to reveal a pop-up box showing various details. **1** Click 'Save to map', **2** choose your map from the drop-down list and click Save. **3**

3 To add new placemarks, click the Placemark button **1**, then click the map to place it and enter a title **2** and a description, switching from Plain to Rich text. **3** Drag the mouse to highlight some text, click the link icon, enter the URL in the pop-up box and click OK, then Done.

4 To add a photo to your description, right-click the image as it appears on the web and select Copy Image URL (or something similar). Next, click on a placemark and select 'Rich text'. Click the photo icon, **1** type Ctrl-V to paste the address into the box and click OK. **2**

5 To add videos from YouTube, paste and embed code into your description, after clicking Edit HTML. **1**

6 Maps can also include lines and shapes, perhaps to mark a route or an area (rather than point) of interest. Click and hold the zigzag icon **1** and release over your choice of line, the line that follows roads or shape. **2**

Combine Ordnance Survey maps with Google

As mapping sites go, it's fair to say that Google has led the way in terms of tools and extras. It still has its limitations, though. Google Maps might be great for drivers, but you can't see footpaths or contours, so you still have to revert back to Ordnance Survey maps if you're on foot. Mapping website Where's the Path (http://wtp2.appspot.com) uses these OS maps, alongside Google's, to bring together the most useful online mapping and information tools in an extremely easy-to-use site.

For hikers and ramblers the route-planning tools are unprecedented. Routes can be exported to GPS devices and easily shared by URL. It not only shows local transport stops, but has all necessary timetables for each, too.

There's also a range of historical maps from the 1930s and 1940s, plus Open Street Map, Google Earth and terrain maps. Each map is capable of displaying relevant Wikipedia entries for towns, villages and landmarks along with images from Panoramio (www.panoramio.com).

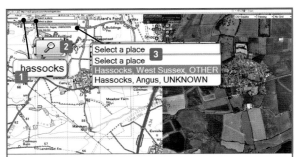

1 Change the location of the map using the box in the top left-hand corner. **1** Type the name of the area you want to browse and click the magnifying glass, **2** and then select the correct location from the drop-down list. **3**

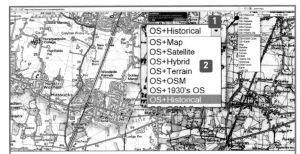

2 You can change the view using the drop-down menu on the right-hand side. **1** You can compare the Ordnance Survey map next to Google Earth, satellite or terrain images, as well as historical maps. **2**

3 To lock a location and get its grid reference, press the padlock icon. **1** Click the precise point on either map you need. **2** Copy the grid reference from the box, **3** and unlock the map by pressing the padlock again.

4 To create a route, select the Route icon, **1** then click along your chosen path, placing nodes on the map at each click. **2** Switch between miles and kilometres by double-clicking the Route text box. **3**

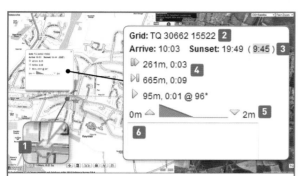

5 Clicking a node **1** will show you its grid reference. **2** This box also shows how far it is from the start and end of the route **3** and distance to the next node. **4** Gradients are shown, too. **5** Add comments in the box underneath. **6**

6 Get the length of your journey by clicking the first, green node on the route. **1** Add the start date and time in the pop-up. **2** Click the last red node to see estimated arrival time. You can also see how long it takes to get to each node.

EXPERT TIP
Any route you create can be exported into GPX and KML files. GPX files can be added to GPS units, while KML is compatible with Google Maps and Earth. Just click the export icon and choose how you want to export. Export to file (not screen) and then upload through your GPS software. With a Garmin satnav, download the Garmin Communicator plug-in, select 'To Garmin' and save directly.

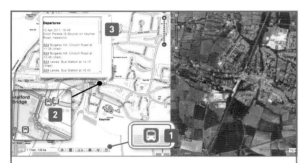

7 Show all local transport stops along your route by pressing the Bus icon. **1** It will show every train and bus stop **2** within 1km of wherever the mouse is clicked. Clicking an icon will then show you times and destinations. **3**

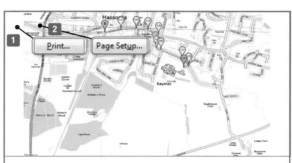

8 Once your route, times and comments are complete, you can print the map to take with you. Press the Print icon and a new tab will open. Go to File and Print. **1** Some maps will need to be changed to landscape in Page Setup. **2**

9 Clicking the W icon **1** will reveal relevant Wikipedia entries for that area. **2** Clicking an icon on the map will show you the entry. **3** Similarly, the compass icon **4** will bring up photos of the area from Panoramio. **5**

10 Sharing a Where's the Path map is easy. Click the Link icon **1** and a URL will appear. **2** Select OK **3** to copy. It saves any view and location preferences, plus routes with comments, which you may want to email to other walkers.

Create your own Google Earth video

Google's virtual globe software (http://earth.google.co.uk) lets you create and share video tours. If you've been on holiday, you can use the software to relive all your adventures, flying from location to location, and returning to all the sights you visited.

You can add descriptions for each place, complete with links and photos, and even record a narration to go with it.

Recorded tours can be saved in Google Earth, exported to your hard disk, emailed and shared online.

Tours don't just have to cover holidays. For inspiration, click the Earth Gallery button in the Layers panel and browse the collection of tours and places that have been created by other Google Earth users. Hover your mouse over a thumbnail to find out more about it.

1 To create a tour, fly to the starting point and zoom in until you're at the right position. Click the Add Placemark icon. **1** A yellow pushpin will appear. **2** Click and drag this into place. Give the location a name. **3**

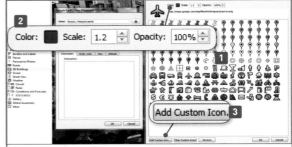

2 You can change the pushpin placement icon to something else by clicking it and selecting one of the alternative choices. **1** You can alter its colour, scale and opacity, too. **2** Click the Add Custom Icon button **3** to add a custom icon.

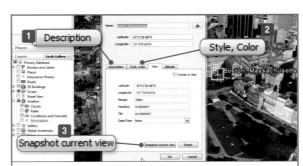

3 You can enter a description **1** for the location, use HTML and add links. Style, Color **2** lets you change the colour, size and opacity of the label and icon. Click 'Snapshot current view' **3** to save it.

4 Click OK and your first stop will be added to the My Places panel. **1** If you need to make changes, right-click the entry and select Properties. Right-click My Places and select Add, Folder. Give it a name and description. **2**

5 Drag the first place into your folder. **1** Fly to your next destination, create a placemark for it, and save it to the folder. When you've finished, click on the folder. You'll see a Play Tour icon. **2** Click this to begin your tour.

6 Google Earth will now fly you from location to location. A set of controls at the bottom left will let you pause, resume, rewind and fast-forward through the locations. **1** The controls will fade out of view when not in use.

7 Adjust the speed of the tour by going to Tools, **1** Options and clicking the Touring tab. **2** Use the sliders **3** to change the length of time between features.

8 Click the 'Record a Tour' (camera) icon. **1** This will open the recording tools. Zoom out to the 'world view', then click the Record button. **2** Explore the first location, then click the next stop in your folder to fly there.

9 The Audio button **1** lets you add a narration. When you finish recording your tour, click the Record button again and Google Earth will play it back. Click the Save icon **2** and give the tour a name. It will appear in the My Places panel.

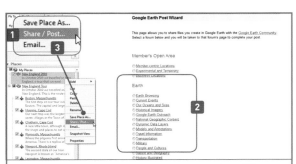

10 To share your tour, right-click it. Share/Post **1** will let you upload it to one of the Google Earth Community forums. **2** Email **3** will let you send the tour, as a KMZ attachment, via Gmail or your default email program.

EXPERT TIP
Google Earth will automatically save any tours you create so they are available the next time you open the program (you can also go to File, Save, Save My Places). If you want to export your creation for safekeeping, or to open on another computer, right-click the tour or folder and select Save Place As. It will be saved as a Google Earth KMZ file.

The Ultimate Guide to
Google's Hidden Tools

Chapter 6
Use Gmail better

Unlock Gmail's hidden tools 56

Secret Gmail tips and tricks 58

Top 10 Gmail add-ons 65

Back up Gmail to your hard disk 67

Gmail shortcuts 68

**Move your Hotmail
account to Gmail** 69

Unlock Gmail's hidden tools

How to boost Gmail using its best and most sophisticated tools

Google's email service lets you do much more than simply send and receive messages. It offers a wealth of powerful features and its Labs section is home to a range of experimental add-ons that let you introduce new elements and customise existing ones. Here, we'll look at some of the more advanced options available.

Gmail Labs tools

In 2011, Google moved three of its more popular Gmail Labs features to the main service, making them integral rather than experimental tools.

First off, there's Superstars, which lets you flag messages with a choice of different icons. Just keep clicking the white star next to an email until you arrive at the one you want. If you don't like any of the choices on offer, click the cog in the top-right corner. Go to 'Mail settings', select the General tab, and choose one of the presets. Alternatively, you can drag icons from 'Not in use' to 'In use', or vice versa.

Another Labs feature, Nested Labels, lets you organise your messages within existing labels, which is a bit like creating a folder within a folder. Hover your mouse over an existing label, click the arrow, and select 'Add sublabel'.

Thirdly, there's Advanced IMAP Controls. This is designed to provide additional features for anyone accessing the service via email software (such as Thunderbird) or a portable device. To access it, go to 'Mail settings', then 'Forwarding and POP/IMAP'.

Add gadgets

The 'Add any gadget by URL' feature found in Labs (which can be accessed through 'Mail settings') lets you add various gadgets to Gmail, including a calendar (http://bit.ly/gcal272), calculator (http://bit.ly/gcalc272), currency converter (http://bit.ly/gcurr272) and URL shortener (http://bit.ly/gurl272).

To install one or more of these, enable the feature in Labs, then go to 'Mail settings', Gadgets. Enter the URL and click Add. You can find additional gadgets to install at www.google.com/ig/directory.

Use the people widget

If you're having an email conversation with several people at the same time, the people widget bar on the right will show you who's involved. There are one-click buttons to email the group or schedule a meeting with them in Google Calendar. Click a sender's name to see recent messages from that person. Alternatively, you can send

them a separate email or start a chat. You can also edit their contact details.

Switch to the mobile interface

There's a special two-pane Gmail interface designed specifically for use on tablets like the iPad. But if you use Chrome, you can try it out with a simple hack. Make a copy of your Chrome shortcut icon, right-click it and select Properties. Go to the end of the text in the Target box, add a space and then type:

```
--user-agent="Mozilla/5.0(iPad; U; iPhone
OS 3_2; en-us) AppleWebKit/531.21.10
Mobile/7B314" --user-data-dir="%tmp%\gmipad"
```

Click Apply and OK. Now launch Chrome from the new shortcut and when you open Gmail (or any other supported service, including Google+), you'll be presented with the new interface. Instead of typing the above code, Copy it from http://bit.ly/gipad272.

Change the style of emails you send

You can specify the default look of any emails you send. Go to 'Mail settings', Labs and enable Default Text Styling. Click Save Changes and go to 'Mail settings', General and locate

the 'Default text style' option. You'll be able to change the typeface, size and text colour, and use bold and italics. The preview window shows you what the changes will look like. To revert to the default settings, click Remove Formatting.

Turn emails into documents

The 'Create a Document' option in Labs lets you turn any message in your inbox into a document in Google Docs, ready for editing, sharing and collaborating on. Once you've enabled it, open a message and select 'Create a document' under More.

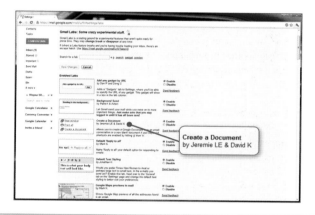

MINI WORKSHOP | Choose an inbox style

1 Gmail offers a choice of ways to organise your inbox, so you can choose the one that suits you best. You can switch between Classic, Important First, Unread First, Starred First and Priority Inbox. Just click your selection in the 'Try on a new inbox' bar. **1** The changes will be made instantly. You can close the bar when it's not required.

2 If you want to change to a different style and the bar isn't available (it automatically disappears after you've used one of the pre-set options for a period of time), click the down arrow next to the Inbox label **1** and make your choice there. You can also change inboxes by going to 'Mail settings' and clicking the Inbox tab. **2**

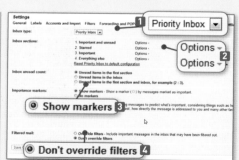

3 The Inbox Settings screen lets you customise the sections on offer and remove any unwanted ones. Pick an Inbox type from the drop-down box, **1** then click the Options link next to a section. **2** You can show or hide the importance markers **3** and choose whether or not to include filtered messages in your inbox. **4**

Secret Gmail tips and tricks

Gmail has loads of tools to improve your messaging experience. Here are 34 tips and tricks for making the most of Google's webmail

Although Gmail has only been publicly available since 2007 – 10 years after the launch of Hotmail or Yahoo Mail – it's quickly become the service of choice for savvy webmail users. The email service's powerful, automatic spam filters, simple interface and increasingly generous storage have won it millions of fans worldwide, while companies as big as Sky (www.sky.com) have adopted it as their default email provider.

Here, we reveal over 30 clever ways to make the most of Gmail. These include tips for enhancing your email, managing your mailbox and strengthening security.

ENHANCE YOUR EMAIL
Drag and drop attachments
If you use Firefox or Chrome, there's no need to click the 'Attach a file' button when you want to send documents and

files to someone. Simply drag and drop the files onto the message to attach them.

Change your message font
You can change the default font for your Gmail messages using the Default Text Styling tool in Labs. Enable the feature, go into Settings and use the toolbar options in the

'Default text style' section to set the font, size and colour of your Gmail messages.

Create a personal signature
You can customise your Gmail messages by adding a signature that contains contact details, web addresses and an image. Go into Settings, scroll down to Signature and choose the second option. Type the information you want

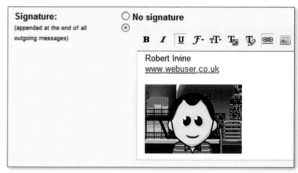

to include, click the Insert Image icon and paste the web address of the picture. Click OK, then Save Changes.

Preview photos in emails
Rather than clicking links to view photos hosted on Flickr and Picasa, you can have Gmail display them in the message itself. Go into Gmail Labs and enable the options 'Flickr previews in mail' and 'Picasa previews in mail' to display pictures automatically at the bottom of emails.

Get extra emoticons
If you're a fan of emoticons, you can access a massive range of colourful characters by enabling the Extra Emoji feature in Labs (http://bit.ly/labs 58). To use them in an email, just click the Insert Emoticon icon on the toolbar.

MANAGE YOUR MAILBOX

Get Desktop alerts for new email

If you use Chrome, you can get pop-up notifications on your Desktop every time you receive a new email. Go to Settings,

click the 'Click here to enable desktop notifications for Gmail' link and click Allow. You can stop receiving Desktop alerts by selecting 'Mail notifications off'.

Sign into two accounts at once

If you've got more than one Gmail account – personal and work, for example – there may be times when you want to have them both open in the same browser. You can set this up by changing your Google Accounts (www.google.com/accounts) settings – see our Mini Workshop below.

Combine labels with filters

Once you've created a coloured label, you can set up a filter to apply it automatically to messages from a particular

person or to emails that contain a specific word. You can then scan new mail just by looking at the colours. Go into Settings, Filters and click 'Create a new filter' and enter some search criteria. Click Next Step, select 'Apply a label', choose your coloured label from the drop-down menu and click Create Filter.

Preview messages without opening

An experimental tool called Message Sneak Peek lets you

preview the content of your messages without having to open them. Enable the feature in Labs, then right-click an email in your inbox or another folder for an instant preview. ▶

MINI WORKSHOP | Switch between two Gmail accounts

1 To sign into two Gmail accounts in the same browser simultaneously, first go to the Google Accounts page (www.google.com/accounts). In the Personal Settings section, find the 'Multiple sign-in' option and click the Edit link. **1**

2 On the next page, ignore the warning that this is an advanced feature **1** and choose the option 'On – Use multiple Google Accounts in the same web browser'. **2** Tick the boxes **3** to show you understand how to use the feature, then click Save.

3 Click the Back link at the top of the page and then return to your Gmail inbox. Now click your username **1** and choose 'Switch account' **2** to switch between your accounts.

Get mail from other accounts

In addition to your Gmail messages, you can read email from up to five POP3 accounts, such as Hotmail, in the same place. Go to Settings, 'Accounts and Import' and click the 'Add POP3 email account' button. Enter the email address of an account you want to import messages from, specify your mail settings and click Add Account.

Apply coloured labels to emails

Gmail's Labels feature provides an excellent means of managing your Inbox by tagging your messages with keywords. You can make emails even easier to find by giving them brightly coloured labels. Click the arrow next to a label in the left-hand menu for a choice of colours, or click 'Add custom colour' for further options.

Find old attachments

If you're looking for an attachment that someone once sent you, Gmail's advanced search operators can help you find what you're looking for quickly and easily. Type 'has:attachment' (without the quotes) into the search box to show all emails with attachments. If you can remember who sent you the message, type 'from:[name] has:attachment' to filter the results.

CONTROL YOUR SENDING

Stop sent messages being delivered

If you change your mind about sending a message as soon as you've clicked Send, don't panic. Go into Labs, enable the option Undo Send and click Save Changes. By default,

Google delays the sending of all messages for 10 seconds, but you can increase this to 20 or 30 seconds. To stop a message being sent, just click Undo.

Send email from another address

Gmail lets you list one of your other email addresses as the sender of an email so you can have all replies directed there. This is useful when you're composing emails on the move but want people to send their replies to your work or home email addresses – see our Mini Workshop opposite.

Read and write messages offline

If you have an unreliable internet connection or a tight monthly data cap, Gmail lets you access your email and compose messages offline. Go to Settings, click the Offline tab and choose 'Enable Offline Mail for this computer'. Decide what you want to download before you go offline – for example, just your Inbox messages – and the maximum attachment size, then click Save Changes.

Pause sending emails you might regret

Mail Goggles is a Labs tool that stops you sending emails while you're drunk that you may later regret. Enable the feature and, if you try to send an email between 10pm and 4am on a Friday or Saturday night, you'll be made to solve maths sums before the message can leave your inbox.

Make sure you've got the right recipient

The Gmail Labs feature 'Got the wrong Bob?' stops you including the wrong people in group emails by identifying names that don't usually go together. So if you've got a

friend and a work colleague with the same first name, Gmail will make sure you address the email to the right person.

Send automatic replies

If you often send the same reply to people, save yourself time and typing by creating a 'canned response'. Enable the Canned Responses feature in Labs and click the 'Compose mail' button. Type the text you want to include in your automatic reply, click the 'Canned responses' menu and choose 'New canned response'. Type a name for the response and you'll be able to select this next time you haven't got time to write a reply.

Ensure everyone gets included

There's a feature called 'Don't forget Bob' that prevents you from omitting people from group emails. Once you pick some email recipients, Gmail will suggest more contacts to include based on the groups of people you email most often.

Write email in a separate window

Another tool is the ability to compose email in a separate window to your browser. Click the arrow icon in the top-right

corner of a 'Compose mail' message window and the email will open in a pop-up window. Alternatively, hold down Shift when you click the 'Compose mail' button. If you use Chrome, the window will remain open even if you close the main browser.

CUSTOMISE GMAIL

Turn off Labs features

Because the tools in Gmail Labs are experimental, there is a chance they may conflict with one another and stop the webmail service working. If you experience problems, you can access your inbox via Gmail's 'safe mode' at http://mail. google.com/mail/?labs=0, which disables all Labs features.

Search Google Docs from Gmail

If you use the excellent online office suite Google Docs (http://docs.google.com), you can find and open files from within Gmail. Just enable the Apps Search feature in Labs and the search box above your Inbox will be renamed 'Search Mail and Docs'.

Apply different themes

If Gmail's interface is too plain for your liking, spice it up with a theme. Go to Settings, then Themes, find a design that suits your taste and click it to apply. In 2011, Google added some great new designs including Android, Tree

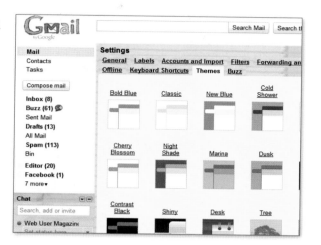

Tops, the hand-drawn Marker and weather-sensitive themes, Bus Stop and Tree.

Make Gmail your default email client

You can have Gmail open every time you click an email link on a website by making it your browser's default email client. In Firefox, go to Tools, Options, Applications, click the 'mailto' entry and choose 'Use Googlemail' from the menu. For Internet Explorer, install the Google Toolbar ▶

MINI WORKSHOP | Send email from a different address

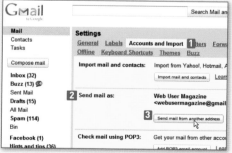

1 If you want to send and receive email using an alternative address, go into Settings and click the 'Accounts and Import' tab. **1** Under your current Gmail address in the 'Send mail as' section, **2** click the 'Send mail from another address' button. **3**

2 On the next screen, type the name you want to use for the alternative address **1** and the email address itself. **2** You can also have messages sent to a third email address by specifying a different reply-to address. Click Next Step **3** to continue.

3 Choose the 'Send through Gmail' option, then click the Send Verification button **1** to confirm the email address. Once you verify it, you can opt to use the alternative address when you're composing messages. Click the drop-down menu next to From: and select it from the available options. **2**

Webuser
The UK's favourite internet magazine

3 ISSUES FOR £1 OFFER

☑ **YES!** Please start my subscription to *Web User* with **3 issues for just £1.** After 3 issues I understand that my subscription will continue by Direct Debit at the **LOW RATE of just £19.99 every 13 issues – saving 23%** on the cover price – unless I write to cancel within my introductory period. If I do cancel, no further money will be taken from my account. The **3 issues for £1** are mine to keep, whatever I decide

Step 1: Complete your details below

Mr/Mrs/Ms   First name

Surname

Job title

Company

Address

                                        Postcode

Daytime tel   Mobile tel

Email   Year of birth (YYYY)

Cheque or Credit/Debit Card

❶ I enclose a cheque made payable to *Dennis Publishing Ltd.*

❷ Credit/Debit card: Please charge my:

☐ VISA ☐ MasterCard ☐ AMEX ☐ Debit/Maestro (Issue No. [____])

Card No. [_____]

Start date (if applicable) [_____]   Expiry date [_____]

Signed   Date

Step 2:

❸ Direct Debit Payment – **Just £1 for 3 issues,** then £19.99 every 13 issues (UK only).

Dennis Instruction to your Bank or Building Society to pay by Direct Debit ● **DIRECT Debit**

Please complete and send to: Freepost RLZS-ETGT-BCZR, Dennis Publishing Ltd, 800 Guillat Ave, Kent Science Park, Sittingbourne ME9 8GU
Name and full postal address of your Bank or Building Society

To the manager: Bank name

Address

                    Postcode

Account in the name(s) of

Branch sort code [__][__][__]

Bank/Building Society account number [_____]

Originator's Identification Number

| 7 | 2 | 4 | 6 | 8 | 0 |

Ref no. to be completed by Dennis Publishing

Instructions to your bank or Building Society
Please pay Dennis Publishing Ltd. Direct Debits from the account detailed in this instruction subject to the safeguards assured by the Direct Debit Guarantee. I understand that this instruction may remain with Dennis Publishing Ltd and, if so, details will be passed electronically to my Bank/Building Society.

Signature(s)

Date

Banks and building societies may not accept Direct Debit instructions for some types of account

---

Dennis Publishing (UK) Ltd uses a layered Privacy Notice, giving you brief details about how we would like to use your personal information. For full details please visit our website **www.dennis.co.uk/privacy/** or call us on **0844 844 0053.** If you have any questions please ask as submitting your details indicates your consent, until you choose otherwise, that we and our partners may contact you about products and services that will be of relevance to you via, direct mail, phone, e-mail and SMS. You can opt-out at ANY time via **www.subsinfo.co.uk** or **privacy@dennis.co.uk** or **0844 844 0053.**

Now return your completed form to:
**Freepost RLZS-ETGT-BCZR,
Web User Subscriptions,
800 Guillat Ave, Kent Science Park,
Sittingbourne ME9 8GU**

(No stamp required)

Offer code: G1120GHT

YOUR GREAT DEAL

★ **3 issues for JUST £1**

★ **SAVE 23%** on the shop price if you continue

★ Pay nothing more if you decide *Web User* isn't for you

★ **FREE delivery** direct to your door

3 issues of Web User
FOR JUST £1

Web User, the UK's favourite internet magazine, is bursting with practical advice to help you get the best out of the web and your PC.

Claim **3 issues for £1** today and get *Web User* delivered free to your door every fortnight.

Inside every issue of Web User you'll find:

▶▶ **NEW Websites** – We bring you the best new and revamped websites on the internet

▶▶ **FREE Software** – We reveal the web's best new software that won't cost you a penny

▶▶ **PC & web tips** – We reveal fantastic tips to help you improve your PC and use the internet better

CALL NOW:
0844 322 1289

Visit **www.dennismags.co.uk/webuser**

using the offer code: G1120GHT

(http://bit.ly/toolbar260), click the spanner icon, go to the Search tab and select 'Use Gmail for 'Mail To' links'. For Chrome, install the extension Send from Gmail (http://bit.ly/chrome260) or Send using Gmail (http://bit.ly/send260).

Use Gmail as an MP3 player
With its generous amount of storage space – more than 7.5GB – Gmail is a great place to back up your music online. Simply attach MP3s to messages and send them to yourself.

The service even lets you listen to your stored tunes – click the Play link next to an audio attachment to play the MP3.

Create a To-do list
Gmail's Tasks feature lets you create a simple To-do list and mark off tasks as they're completed. Click the Tasks option on the left-hand side of the screen to open a pop-up window bottom-right. Click the '+' sign to add a new task and select the box next to a task to mark it as done.

Search Google from Gmail
Gmail already provides a 'Search the web' box, but by enabling the Google Search feature in Labs, you can view Google search results as you compose and read messages. Just type a query into the Web Search box and the results will appear in a pop-up window.

Hide Contacts and Tasks
Gmail's Contacts and Tasks features were added to the top-left corner of the interface when the webmail service was last revamped. To hide these options, click the minus sign next to Mail; to display them again, click the plus sign.

Use secret keyboard shortcuts
The keyboard-shortcuts guide lists plenty of time-saving tips but there are a couple of extra shortcuts to speed up

your sending. Press 'd' to compose a new message with the 'Cc:' field open, so you can add extra recipients, and 'b' to include a 'Bcc:' field to add multiple, hidden recipients. You'll need to turn on keyboard shortcuts first by going to Settings, General and selecting 'Keyboard shortcuts on'.

View Gmail's keyboard shortcuts
Once you've turned keyboard shortcuts on, you can find out what they are by pressing '?' (Shift+/). The reference guide that opens obscures your view so it's best to click 'Open in a new window' and then print it out.

Play a secret game of Snake
With keyboard shortcuts enabled in Gmail, you can unlock a special version of the classic arcade game Snake. First, go into Labs, enable the feature Old Snakey and click Save Changes. Press the '&' key (Shift+7) to launch the game and use the arrow keys to guide your snake around.

Add a 'Mark as Read' button
One of the more fiddly aspects of Gmail is having to click on the 'More actions' menu and select 'Mark as read' when you don't want to read messages. Enable the Mark as Read Button tool in Labs and you'll be able to perform this action with a single click.

Turn off Conversation View
Gmail's Conversation View groups all replies to an email in one message. If you find the feature unfamiliar and confusing, you can turn it off. Go into Settings and, on the General tab, select 'Conversation view off'. Click Save Changes and any replies will appear as separate messages.

Switch to basic HTML view
When Gmail has one of its outages, it's often still possible to access the service via its no-frills, basic HTML view. You can switch to this by clicking the 'basic HTML' link at the bottom of the Gmail page. Add this plain view to your Bookmarks or Favorites and switch back to standard view. Next time Gmail goes down, try this basic HTML version (or just go to http://mail.google.com/mail/?ui=html).

Top 10 Gmail add-ons

As well as Google's own features, there are plenty of third-party tools to enhance your Gmail experience. Here are 10 of the best

Integrated Gmail
www.integratedgmail.com

This clever Firefox add-on lets you collapse your Gmail inbox to access other Google services such as Calendar, Reader and Picasa in one place.

Remember the Milk for Gmail
http://bit.ly/milk260

Remember the Milk's Firefox and Chrome add-on lets you add and manage Gmail tasks on the go and is seamlessly integrated with your contact list and calendar.

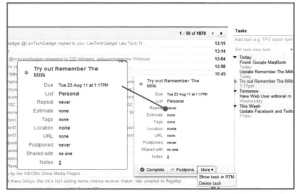

Google Mail Checker Plus
http://chrome.desc.se

Chrome extension Google Mail Checker Plus tells you when you receive new mail, and lets you read, delete and archive messages, without leaving your current tab.

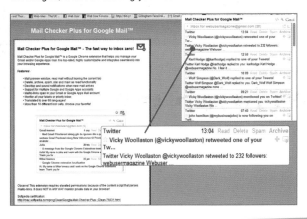

Better Gmail 2
http://bit.ly/better260

This Firefox add-on is packed with useful Gmail enhancements. Our favourite is the option to have a sound alert when you receive new email.

Minimalist for Gmail
http://bit.ly/minimalist260
If you think Gmail's interface has become too cluttered, this Chrome extension can to strip it back.

Gmail Drive
www.viksoe.dk/Gmail
This Windows tool adds Gmail to My Computer as an additional 7.5GB drive. Drag files to it and they will be uploaded to Gmail in the form of an email.

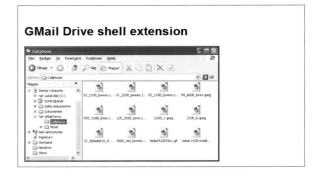

Gmail for Android
www.android.com/ market
Google's Android app uses Priority Inbox to bring your most important messages to the fore.

ActiveInbox
www.activein boxhq.com
This handy browser plug-in for Firefox and Chrome is based on the Getting Things Done (GTD) system. It uses labels to turn your Gmail messages into tasks.

Hide Gmail Ads
http://doiop.com/gmailads
If you find the adverts next to and above Gmail messages distracting, this add-on for Firefox and Chrome gets rid of them and expands your viewing area.

Boomerang for Gmail
www.boomeranggmail.com
Want to write an email now but send it later? The Boomerang add-on for Firefox and Chrome lets you schedule a message to be sent whenever you want.

Back up Gmail to your hard disk

Here's how to create a back-up using Mozilla's Thunderbird email software

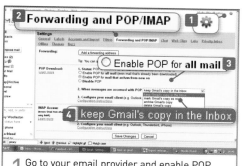

1 Go to your email provider and enable POP access. In Gmail, click the cog icon, **1** choose 'Mail settings', 'Forwarding and POP/IMAP', **2** then 'Enable POP for all mail'. **3** Choose to 'keep Gmail's copy in the Inbox' **4** and press Save Changes.

2 In Thunderbird, go to Tools, **1** Account Settings and, under Account Actions, choose Add Mail Account. Enter your name, email address and email password. Click Continue. Select POP3 **2** to download the files locally – this will create a back-up. Then click Create Account. **3**

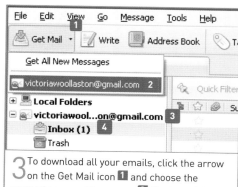

3 To download all your emails, click the arrow on the Get Mail icon **1** and choose the account you want to access. **2** For large inboxes, this may take some time. To view your emails, click the plus sign next to the account name **3** and then Inbox. **4**

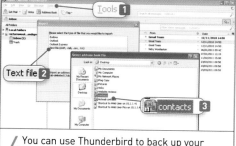

4 You can use Thunderbird to back up your Gmail contacts, too. From Gmail Contacts, choose 'More actions', then Export. Save as 'Outlook CSV format'. In Thunderbird, go to Tools, **1** Import, 'Address books'. Select 'Text file' **2** and open your saved contacts list. **3**

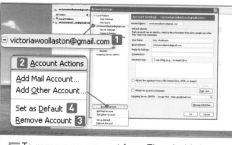

5 To remove an account from Thunderbird, go to Tools, Account Settings, then highlight the relevant account in the left-hand menu. **1** Under Account Actions, **2** choose Remove Account. **3** You can also set an account as the default by choosing 'Set as Default'. **4**

6 For added security, you can back up your whole Thunderbird profile to disk. To find your profile in Windows 7 and Vista, go to Start (Start, then Run, in XP) and type '%APPDATA%\Thunderbird\Profiles\' (without the quotes). **1** Now copy the folder onto an external disk or similar.

Gmail shortcuts

Keyboard shortcuts are much speedier than using a mouse. Here are some extremely useful shortcuts for Gmail

https://mail.google.com

You can get the full list of Gmail shortcut keys by pressing the '?' key. To differentiate between the '?' and '/' on the same key, press Shift. You'll need to turn on keyboard shortcuts in the Mail Settings.

C

The C stands for 'compose' and creates a new message. Pressing Shift+C opens the message in a new window.

Shift+Enter

Once you've written your message, send it by pressing Shift+Enter.

Z

This shortcut will undo the last action anywhere within Gmail. This includes undoing typing and moving messages from one folder to another.

G

To jump between mailbox folders, you can use the following combinations:
G+I for Inbox

G+T for Sent items
G+D for Drafts
G+C for Contacts
G+B for Buzz

O

Use the arrow keys to scroll through your inbox and hit O (the letter) to open a message.

R

Use this shortcut to reply to a message. Pressing A replies to all recipients and F will forward the message.

Ctrl+S

This shortcut saves the message you're writing as a draft.

#

Press the # key or the Delete key to move a message to the Trash folder.

/

The forward-slash key puts your cursor in the Search box, so you can find a particular message.

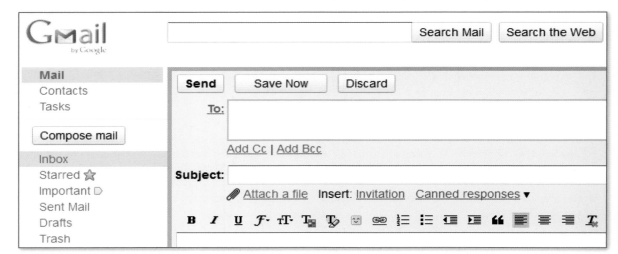

Move your Hotmail account to Gmail

Switching to Gmail is easier than you'd think. Here's how to do it from Hotmail

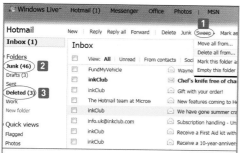

1 Before you transfer your messages, delete any you don't require, such as old newsletters and offers. There's a useful Sweep function **1** that will let you delete all messages from a particular sender. Be sure to empty your Junk **2** and Deleted folders **3** too.

2 To move your remaining messages to Gmail, open a new account and then go to Settings. **1** Click the 'Accounts and Import' tab. **2** This lets you transfer emails from a range of popular services. Click the 'Import mail and contacts' button. **3**

3 A window will open, asking where you want to import your messages from. Enter your Hotmail address and password. Your login details are held by TrueSwitch (Google's partner), but deleted according to your preference after a maximum of 30 days. Choose what to import. **1**

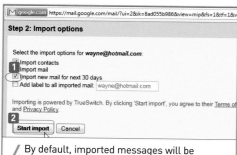

4 By default, imported messages will be labelled with your Hotmail address, so you can see where they've come from. If you don't want this to happen, untick that option. **1** Click 'Start import' **2** and Gmail will go to work. This process can take several hours.

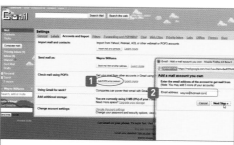

5 Unless you unticked the option, TrueSwitch will copy new Hotmail messages to your Gmail account for the next 30 days. You can extend this period (indefinitely, if you like) by going to 'Accounts and Import' and clicking 'Add POP3 email account'. **1** Enter your Hotmail address. **2**

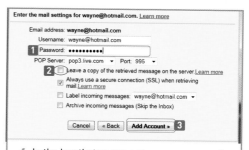

6 In the box that opens, enter your password. **1** The server and port details will be filled in automatically. Tick the option to 'Leave a copy of the retrieved messages on the server' **2** if you want the emails to remain available through Hotmail. Click Add Account. **3**

The Ultimate Guide to
Google's Hidden Tools

Chapter 7
Make Google more secure

Make your Google profile private............................ 72

Protect your Google account from hackers 73

Share photos privately with Picasa 74

How to keep everything private in Google........................... 75

Make your Google profile private

Everyone with a Google account also has a Google Profile – a web page that can reveal as much information about yourself as you choose. Here's how to keep it private

1 Only completed fields are visible on your profile, but it's worth removing things such as maiden and children's names, which you may have used as a password hint or security question on other accounts. Click the 'Edit profile' button **1**, then change/delete any unwanted information.

2 Your birthday and phone numbers are hidden from public view by default. To manage who can see these, click each field in the 'Edit profile' screen. Tick the boxes of the groups **1** you want to share this information with, then click Save. **2**

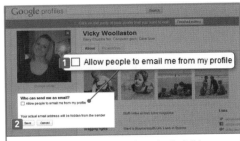

3 Although your email address isn't visible, people can still email you through your connected account. To disable this feature click 'Email is on' under your profile picture and untick the 'Allow people to email me from my profile' box **1** and click Save. **2**

4 Manage linked accounts using the Links box. **1** To edit a connection, click the pencil icon. **2** Click the cross to remove a connection. **3** To just hide the connections select 'Manage connected accounts', **4** then untick the 'Show on my public Google Profile' box.

5 To organise photos added to your profile, click Scrapbook, then 'manage photos'. Under the My Photos tab, **1** click 'Edit visibility'. **2** From the drop-down menu change 'Public on the web' **3** to 'Anyone with the link', **4** so they're visible only to those you allow.

6 Alternatively, if you want to include all this information so that your contacts can see it, but hide your profile from the public, click the 'Search visibility' field and untick the 'Help others find my profile in search results' box. **1** Click Save. **2**

Protect your Google account from hackers

There's so much personal information in your Google account, it's crucial you keep it safe from hackers. We show you how to add extra security layers to your account

1 Google's 2-step verification option adds an extra security level. Once set up, you will need your username, password and a unique code to access your account. To begin set up, go to My Account **1** and, under Personal Settings/Security, click 'Using 2-step verification'. **2**

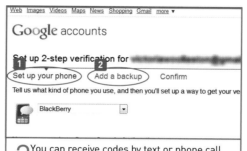

2 You can receive codes by text or phone call. Smartphone users can install the Google Authenticator app by clicking 'Set up your phone'. **1** Every time you access your account, you'll receive a code that can be used for an hour. Create back-up options **2** in case you lose your phone.

3 After setting up 2-step verification, you can generate unique smartphone passwords. In My Account, 'Authorizing applications & sites', enter the name of the application and Google will generate a password. **1** Once your device is verified, you won't have to re-enter the password.

4 Secure your Gmail account further by only accessing it using the 'https' prefix. This keeps your email encrypted, even on unsecured networks. Click 'Mail settings' **1** and, under General, 'Browser connection', select 'Always use https', **2** then Save to activate.

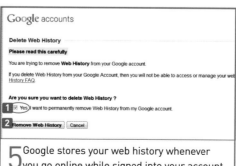

5 Google stores your web history whenever you go online while signed into your account. To stop this, go to My Account, click Edit next to 'My products' and 'Remove Web History permanently'. Tick the box **1** and confirm by clicking Remove Web History. **2**

6 If you forget your password, or suspect that someone is using it to access your account, you can recover or update it. Change it under My Account, 'Changing your password'. Click 'Recovering your password' to reset it and set your recovery options **1** and security question. **2**

Share photos privately with Picasa

If you want to share your photos, Picasa Web Albums is private, secure and simple – especially if you upload via Picasa, Google's handy image organiser

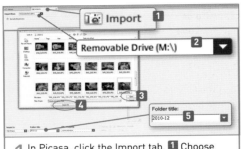

1 In Picasa, click the Import tab. **1** Choose the folder your pictures are kept in from the drop-down menu next to 'Import from:'. **2** Select the images you want and click Open **3** or click Import All. **4** Name the 'Folder title', **5** which becomes the album name, and click Import All again.

2 To prepare and upload the photos for the web, select them and click Upload. **1** The new dialog box shows the default settings. You can change the upload size **2** and select Private from the 'Visibility for this album' drop-down menu. **3** Once you've made any changes, click Upload. **4**

3 Slide the 'Sync to web' slider to the on position, **1** then click Sync **2** in the dialog box. Any changes made to the folder, including the addition of new photos, will be replicated on the web. If you prefer not to install the software, you can upload photos direct to the site.

4 Go to Picasa Web Albums (http://picasaweb. google.com), click the My Photos tab **1** and select the album you want to share. This will open the album, so you can see thumbnails of all the pictures.

5 Click the Edit drop-down menu **1** to organise, edit or rename your albums and pictures. Click Share **2** to let your friends and family access the album.

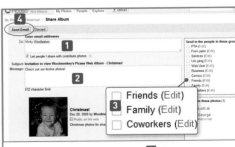

6 Insert the email addresses **1** of anyone you want to send the link to. Add a message **2** if you wish. If you have set up mailing lists for different groups of people, you can send a single mail to everyone in the group by selecting that group. **3** Click 'Send Email'. **4**

How to keep everything private in Google

Google is often criticised for its privacy policies, but most of its products feature settings that help protect your personal data. We explain how to find and enable them

Gmail
https://mail.google.com

To protect your Gmail inbox and contacts, make sure you only ever access your account on a secure server, whatever computer you're using. Go into Mail Settings and, on the General tab, choose the option 'Always use https' in the 'Browser connection' option section. This will guarantee that you always log in using a secure server, even on public and unsecured networks.

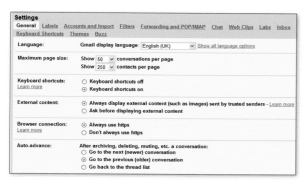

If you want to give someone else access to your Gmail account without revealing your password, go to 'Accounts and Import' under Settings, click the 'Add another account' link next to 'Grant access to your account' and enter their email address. They won't be able to change your settings.

YouTube
http://uk.youtube.com

To keep your YouTube videos private, sign into the site, click the arrows next to your Account name and choose Settings. The Privacy tab lets you choose who can send and share your videos, as well as what statistics and data linked with your account are made visible to the public. Click Manage

Account if you want to change either your password or the Google account that's associated with your YouTube account, and set which third-party sites and apps can access your information.

To prevent people from seeing what you've been watching, click the Sign Out Everywhere link at the bottom of the page to sign out of all YouTube sessions on any computer or device.

Web History

Each time you make a search while signed into your Google account, the details are stored. This search history is then used to personalise future search results. You can delete your entire history by clicking the gear icon on any page in your Google account. Choose Account Settings, Web History then 'Clear entire web history'.

You can also access this setting from Google search results by clicking 'View customisations' at the bottom of the page. Rather than clearing the entire history, you can also delete individual results under 'Manage web history'. Choose the tick boxes next to the unwanted entries, then click Remove.

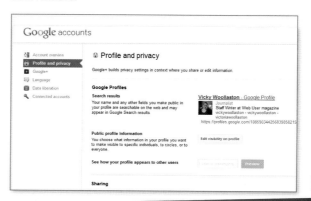

►

Google+
https://plus.google.com

Google+ has already been praised for its robust default privacy options. You can tighten the security further by choosing 'Google+ settings' from the Gear menu when viewing your profile.

The Google+ tab manages your notification options and delivery preferences, and lets you set the location preferences on your photos. The 'Profile and privacy' setting lets you edit your circles, including who can share posts with you and who your posts are shared with. Your network visibility, which shows the other people that appear on your profile, can also be edited here. The last circle with which you shared content is set as the default, which can't be changed, but you can decide how your photos are shared, regardless of the circle.

Picasa Web Albums
https://picasaweb.google.com

To stop unauthorised people viewing the pictures you upload to Picasa Web Albums, click the 'edit' link in the information section for a particular album and set the Visibility to

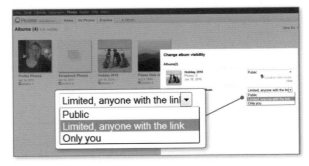

Limited or 'Only you'. Alternatively, you can change the privacy settings of multiple albums by clicking the 'Edit visibility' link on the main Albums page.

For further privacy controls, choose 'Photos settings' in the Gear menu, then click the 'Privacy and Permissions' tab. Here, you can stop Picasa automatically mapping photos if they contain location data and also prevent people from ordering and downloading your photos.

Google +1
www.google.com/+1/button

Clicking a Google +1 link lets you share pages you like or are interested in with other people. Google stores these pages on the +1 tab in your Google account by accessing your profile and holding details of the URL you +1ed, your IP address and information about your browser.

To stop Google saving this data, you can undo the +1 option by going to the list of sites you've recommended and clicking Undo. The information is then deleted. If you don't want to see +1 recommendations on third-party sites, you can disable them at http://bit.ly/plusone274. And if you don't want others to see your recommendations, go to the +1 tab on your profile and untick the 'Show this tab on your profile' box. The +1 information can only be shared if your profile is publicly visible. To change this, go to 'Account settings', 'Account overview', 'Edit profile' and deselect the 'Search visibility' option.

Google advertising
www.google.co.uk/ads

When you search using Google, your history and site visits are tracked using cookies such as DoubleClick. This helps Google show you targeted ads, based on what you've searched for previously. Aside from deleting your web history, you can manage your advertising settings by opting out of the DoubleClick cookie in the Privacy Center (http://bit.ly/optout274). If you don't want to opt out completely, click 'Manage your ads preferences' on the same page to select which ads you see.

To edit advert preferences on Android devices, Google provides a QR code at http://bit.ly/androidads274 that lets you manage the settings, or you can download the Google Search app and edit your preferences from there. You can also install an opt-out plug-in for Firefox, IE and Chrome (http://bit.ly/adsplugin274)

Google Street View
http://bit.ly/streetview274

If you find that Google's Street View technology has failed to blur a face or a number plate, or you want part of an image blurred to protect your privacy, such as your house or car, you can report the image in question to Google. Find the image in Street View, click the 'Report a problem' link in the bottom-left corner of the page and fill out the form that opens. Google reviews the image in light of the information you've provided and will get back to you with a decision as soon as it can.

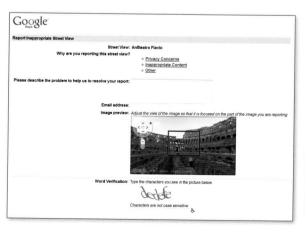

Google Docs
https://doc.google.com

By default, Google makes documents stored within Docs only visible to you. To manage who you share your documents with, select one from your list using the tick boxes, click the arrow button in the top-right corner to show the Details pane and click the pencil icon next to Sharing. Add or remove the people who have access or manage how they access it; whether they can edit or just view. In the Actions drop-down menu, you can also hide selected documents from the homepage or download them all.

Google Calendar
http://calendar.google.com

You can choose to share only certain elements of your Google calendar with other people, which is handy if you use it to organise both your personal and business timetable. Choose 'Calendar settings' from the Gear menu, then

decide whether to make the calendar public or only visible to certain people. You can enter their email addresses below. From the Permission Settings menu, choose whether each person can see all your events or just information about whether you're free or busy on a particular day. You can also set whether they can edit your events.

Chapter 8

Get more traffic to your site

Master Google's
Webmaster tools 80

Giving your website
the local touch 84

Master Google's Webmaster tools

Google provides tools to help you optimise your website so others can get more from it. We explain how to hammer your site into shape

Getting your website to appear in Google search results is one of the best ways to start building a community or business on the internet. To add a site to the Google index, you need to go to http://google.co.uk/addurl and provide Google with the full URL to your site. It's free, and within a few days your site should start appearing in search results.

The search giant uses a number of different methods for ranking websites, so it can be difficult trying to work out why your site is not appearing as a top result, or even at all, in relevant searches. This has led to the development of many strategies for exploiting loopholes in search engines to boost your position in search results. Generally, this involves trying to deceive the Google indexing service, by providing different content to search engines than to users. Another strategy is to take part in link-sharing schemes, attempting to abuse the fact that Google ranks well-linked sites more highly than other similar ones. You should avoid tricks of this type, though; if Google detects you are playing the system, it can reduce your site's ranking or even remove it from the index.

The Dashboard includes the top searches that your website featured as a result

This is where the Webmaster Tools service is invaluable, as it gives you an insight into how Google is viewing your website, allowing you to fix problems and optimise your search ranking. Using Webmaster Tools will also help your website's ranking in other search engines such as Yahoo, because many of the rules for Google apply equally well to them.

To start using Google Webmaster Tools, go to www.google.com/webmasters/tools and sign in with your existing Google Account; you can sign up for one first if you don't have one. After logging in, you need to add your website so that you can start using the tools. To do this, you have to click the 'Add a site' button and type in the full URL of your website. For security reasons you need to prove to Google that you really are the owner of the website. This is most easily done by uploading a verification file to your website's root folder. Once this is done, you can access the Dashboard and start using the tools to optimise your website.

Making a dash for it

After logging in to Webmaster Tools and selecting your site, you're taken to the Dashboard. This shows a brief overview of how well your website is indexed by Google as well as any urgent errors. If this is the first time you've used the tools after adding your site to Google, the Dashboard will be empty as data won't have been collected yet. It may take a few days for useful data to start appearing.

It's worth taking a few minutes to look at the Dashboard when you log in as it can help to keep your site optimised. The screen is divided into several reports, each of which has a more detailed and in-depth tool that can be accessed from links on the left of the page. In particular, it's worth reviewing the Search queries and Keywords reports. These give an indication of the searches that found your website and the keywords that Google has identified from analysing the content of your pages.

The Crawl errors report shows feedback from Google for any problems that were encountered when indexing pages from your site. This includes problems with dynamic content such as failing PHP scripts, but more commonly it's from broken hyperlinks in your pages. It's important to fix these things as quickly as possible: visitors don't like broken links on sites and Google can't index pages that it cannot reach. After reading the overview, you can start using the 'Site

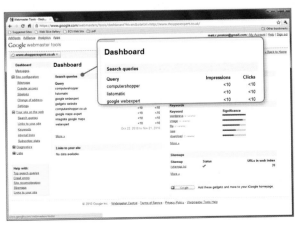

configuration' tools to optimise the way Google accesses and indexes the content in your website.

Map reading

One of the biggest problems you'll encounter when adding a site to Google is that certain pages might not show up in the search results at all. This can happen as the Google indexing service locates pages to index by following links from within the content of your pages. If some pages aren't reachable, have links that are created dynamically by a script or are part of a Flash movie, then Google won't be able to locate them. Sitemaps can solve this by providing a list of all the pages in your website.

In its most basic form, a Sitemap is a text file with a list or URLs to pages in your website, one per line. This is enough to inform Google about the pages available on your website. When making the Sitemap, you need to make sure that you specify all URLs consistently. So if, for example, you registered your site as www.shopperexpert.co.uk, you should ensure that all URLs in the Sitemap begin with www.shopperexpert.co.uk/. When you've created the sitemap, make sure it's named with a .txt file extension and upload it to your website. Then, in Webmaster tools, select the Submit a Sitemap button and enter the path you used.

If you have a very large website, you need to make sure that your Sitemap does not exceed 50,000 entries. If it does, split it into several smaller files and submit them separately. You can reduce the size of your Sitemap files by creating Zip files of them, but the limit of the number of URLs per file still stands.

There is a more descriptive format for Sitemap files that lets you specify more about the pages and assets in your website, using an XML format. This style of Sitemap allows you to annotate resources such as images and videos with subjects and running times. Adding this metadata for images is particularly useful for good integration into Google image searches. There are plenty of websites that will attempt to automatically generate XML Sitemaps – for example, www.xml-sitemaps.com.

Call off the search

The opposite problem is when you have content in your website that you don't want to appear in search results – for instance, confidential or out-of-date information. This is where crawler access tools come in useful. The method for preventing URLs being added to the search index is to create a file named 'robots.txt' in the root directory of your website. This file contains instructions to search engines about which files and directories they're allowed to process. The syntax of this file can be a bit confusing, but Webmaster Tools has a 'Generate robots.txt' utility to help you out.

In most cases, it's best to start by selecting 'Allow all' for the default crawler access. Disabling this would prevent your website appearing in any search results. You can then use a series of block actions to exclude specific URLs from being indexed and appearing in search results. Select 'All robots' to block all search engines. When you have finished adding block rules, click the download button to download the finished robots.txt file. You then need to upload the file to the root directory of your website.

Webmaster Tools also includes a utility to test your robots.txt file, to make sure that it's working as you expect. To try this, select the 'Test robots.txt' tab and paste the contents of your robots.txt file into the box. Click the Test button to see the results. You can also experiment with changes to your robots.txt here. When you're happy with the changes, make sure you update the contents of robots.txt on your website with the new settings.

The missing links

Sitelinks are shown below some websites in Google search results. They make it easier for users to navigate your site from search results – for example, by going straight to the download or support page. Google creates these links by analysing the structure of your website.

Although there isn't currently any way of creating these links in Webmaster tools, there's a simple guideline for helping Google to discover the structure of your website. Ensure that important pages in your website are always available within one or two clicks from the homepage. Also, if users arrive at a page in your site from a search engine, make sure they can navigate to the homepage and the main sections easily. With this structure in place, Google should be able work out relevant sitelinks for your website.

In the rare off chance that Google has made a mistake and created a sitelink for a section of your website that you don't want to appear in search results, you can remove it by using Webmaster tools. Using the

You can exclude certain pages of your website appearing in search results using robots.txt

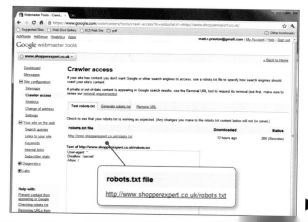

Sitelinks section in Webmaster tools, select the sitelink you would like to remove and then click the Block button.

Change of address

If, for some reason, you need to change the domain name of your website, Webmaster Tools provides a tool for telling Google about the new URL. There is a series of steps to follow that can help Google to update its indexes faster and make the transition smoother for your visitors.

After setting up your site at the new domain, you must make sure that you add it to your Webmaster tools account and verify that you are the owner. Next, you need to redirect all traffic from the old site to the new one. If your site is using the Apache web server, you can do this by setting up an HTTP redirect in an .htaccess file. Finally, using the 'Change of address' tool, tell Google that your site has moved from one address to another.

Search party

The Search queries tool provides details on the top Google search queries that return results containing pages from your website. By default, the top queries from the past 30 days are shown, although the date range used is configurable. Three key pieces of information are shown: Queries, Impressions and Clicks. These values are related to how many search queries contained pages from your website, how many were viewed and how many were clicked on. Impressions and Clicks also show the percentage increase and decrease over the previous time period, so you can see how your website it developing. In all cases, higher numbers and increasing averages are better, as it means that your website is frequently appearing in searches and is well ranked.

Review the most relevant keywords identified by Google from your website

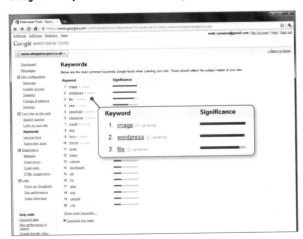

You can also view information about each of the top queries to see how many impressions and visits to your site each one has generated. Each query shows your page's average position in the search result for that query. The higher the position, the greater the chance that it is being viewed and clicked, which, in turn, will lead to people visiting your website. By default, this view shows queries found

from all Google searches, but by using the Filters button you can narrow the results to a specific search type, such as mobile, image or web. The Top Pages tab shows similar statistics, but allows you to narrow the data for individual pages within your website.

Analysing the top queries can help you to improve the content of your site. In conjunction with this, you can use the Keywords tool to see the top keywords that Google has identified from your website. Clicking on any of the keywords will show more details, such as the number of occurrences and the variations. Google can identify spelling variations, including plurals – such as 'image' and 'images' – and group them together. If a keyword isn't ranked as highly as you expected, this suggests that your content needs more work to make it more relevant.

The links effect

In order to work out the relevancy of search results, Google will measure how well a website is linked to from others. The 'Links to your site' section shows an overview of how well your website is linked, where those links are coming from and which are your most linked pages. This is useful data to track as it directly influences your search ranking and the availability of links to your website.

The Internal links section shows a slightly different aspect: the links between pages in your own website. Each page that has internal links to it can be clicked on to show details of where the links are from. Google uses this information in its relevancy calculations. If important pages do not appear in this list, or have far fewer links than other less important pages, you may need to reorganise your link structure. Use this tool before renaming pages to prevent creating broken links in your website.

Secret service

Google is also able to detect malware, which is any software designed to secretly access computer information without the user's consent. If found, Google will provide detailed information in the Malware section of Google Webmaster Tools. If your website has been hacked, it can be used to host viruses, worms and spyware. To protect users, Google will mark search results that point to infected sites, warning users about the potential dangers of visiting them.

If your site has been infected with malware, you'll need to take immediate steps. First, you should take your website offline to prevent the malware from spreading. You should then update all your passwords and set about removing the malware. If your website is small, this could be as simple as looking for new pages or suspicious content that has been added. The larger the website, the more difficult this process is. If you have a recent back-up, it's probably best to replace your live site with that. If your website is based on a CMS such as WordPress, Joomla or Drupal, consider checking online for the latest updates and security fixes.

After you have removed the malicious code, you can request that Google reviews your site by clicking on the 'Request a review' link. Google will check your website and if doesn't find any malware, the malware warnings will be removed from search results to your website.

Forward crawl

The 'Crawl errors' and 'Crawl stats' sections provide feedback from Googlebot, which is the tool Google uses for downloading content from your website to build its search index. Crawl errors are created whenever Googlebot is unable to download pages, usually because of broken links. The Crawl errors tool lists all the broken links found so that you can correct them; broken links annoy users and prevent Google indexing your content.

Crawl stats are useful to check as they can show you how frequently Google is visiting your site to check for updated content. As you improve your website, add new pages and gain in popularity, Google will increase the frequency of visits to index your content.

Language barriers

The 'HTML suggestions' tool shows information about any HTML problems Google found while indexing your website. These problems won't prevent your website being indexed, but they can affect the descriptions of any web pages that appear in search results. Problems detected tend to fall into three categories: Title, Metadata description and non-indexable content.

Snippets of web pages that appear in search results are generated automatically, but where possible they include the title and description from the <title> and <meta name="description"> tags in the HTML. Google will make suggestions about these tags if they are missing, too short or long, or duplicated between pages. Pages that include non-indexable content, such as some rich media, are reported here for your information.

Lab work

Google's Labs section has been a valuable testing ground for experimental new tools. However, Google announced in mid-2011 that it plans to phase out Labs, integrating

Use Google Page Speed to fix performance problems

the best tools elsewhere. Hopefully, this will mean that 'Fetch as Googlebot', a utility that allows you to check the content Google is seeing from your website when it's being indexed will survive. Type in the URL for a page in your website to see the content Google is going to download when indexing. This can be useful when you're making changes to your site, and for checking that your site

is clean after removing malware. It can also be useful as a method for checking that URLs forbidden in your robots.txt are being blocked correctly.

Performance artist

The 'Site performance' section displays the average load times for pages in your website over the past few months. The page-load time is calculated as the total time between when the user clicks on the link in their browser to when the page is fully loaded.

This information is automatically collected from users who have installed the Google Toolbar and enabled the PageRank feature. Improving your page-load times is useful, as people will avoid slow sites.

Besides paying to increase the bandwidth for your site, there are other ways to improve performance. Adding GZIP compression can make web pages smaller, reducing the transfer time and making them load faster.

Several browser plug-ins can analyse the performance of your site and offer suggestions. Google Page Speed (http://code.google.com/speed/page-speed) and Yahoo YSlow (http://developer.yahoo.com/yslow) are free open-source Firefox browser extensions. Both provide a set of best practices that can drastically improve the performance of your website. Finally, the Video Sitemap section shows the errors found while processing these specialised Sitemaps. Video sitemaps are specialised for describing the details of videos on your website, including their duration and subject. These can get complicated, so this tool can help to validate them.

Giving your website the local touch

It's important you ensure visitors find the services relevant to their location. Here, we show you how to use Google's local search engine

If you can get your website to appear on the right local searches, you'll find an increased amount of relevant traffic flowing to it. If you're running your own business, this is crucial. Here, we'll show you how to ensure that your site is appearing on the right searches.

When Google works out where a website is based, it uses a wide range of features. Getting a match on as many as possible will ensure that you get the most relevant visitors. One of the primary sources Google uses is your website's domain name. For sites in the United Kingdom, a '.uk' domain name, such as those ending in '.co.uk', should be considered an essential. It immediately tells Google your website is aimed at people in Britain. This should help your site appear in the www.google.co.uk rankings, particularly when people select the 'Pages from the UK' link.

Google Places lets you add lots of information about your business, making it easy for people to find

There are, however, other factors. Where your web host has its servers is also crucial, as Google can identify their location by the server's IP address. That's not to say that all web hosts with foreign data centres are bad, though – 1&1 Internet has servers hosted in Germany, but customers that order a site through the UK website are given a UK IP address. As far as Google is concerned, your 1&1 website is located in England, even if it's physically stored in Germany.

If you've bought your domain and hosting through a foreign website, your website could appear in the wrong local search engine results. If this is the case, you should consider moving your website to a UK hosting company. It may cost a bit more per year, but the gains you'll get from more customers will probably be worth it in the long run.

You should also tell Google exactly where your website is located: the more information you give, the better the result. Go to www.google.co.uk/addurl. This submission service lets you tell Google that your website exists and should be added to the index, so that people can search for it. Just type in the full address of your website, including the 'http://', and add a comment explaining what your site's about, type in the CAPTCHA and click Add URL. The next page will tell you that your site has been added. Google makes no promises about when your website will start to appear in search results, or if it ever will. That said, provided your site has relevant information stored on it, Google should accept it into its search engine.

Pinpoint accuracy

One of the best ways to tell Google where you're located is to use the Webmaster Tools to set a geographic target for your website. This tells Google which country your site is based in, although you can only apply this information to non-specific domains such as '.com', as '.co.uk' addresses are assumed to be country-specific. To set a Geo Location, go to www.google.com/webmasters/tools. You'll need to log in with your existing Google Account, but you can click the 'Create an account now' link if you don't have one.

Once you've logged into your account, you'll need to add your website before you can use any of the tools. To do this, click the 'Add a site' button and type in the URL of your site. Click Continue when you're done. On the next page, you'll be asked to verify that you're the owner of your website. If this step wasn't in place, other people would be able to make changes to how Google sees your website, which could prove disastrous. Until you've taken this step, you'll be unable to use the tools properly.

There are a few options you can use to verify your site, each with their own instructions. Probably the easiest method is to select 'Upload an HTML file to your server'. This requires you to download a verification HTML file and upload it to your website's root folder. Once you've chosen your method and followed the instructions, click the Verify button to have your site verified.

Tools gold

Google's Webmaster Tools provide a lot of extra tools and features that you can use to manage your website, find out which search terms are driving people to your site, and more besides. The main feature that the Webmaster Tools allow you to do is set your website's country. Click on your website from the Webmaster Tools main page, expand the 'Site configuration' section on the left-hand side, then click on Settings. Tick the 'Target users in' option and select your country from the drop-down list. Click Save to apply the settings. It may take a while, but your website should start appearing on the local search results.

Return of the map

While the above steps should help ensure that your website appears on the correct local search results, there's another way for people to find businesses through the search giant: Google Maps. The integrated search means people can find an area and search it for businesses. It's important, then, that your business appears correctly on the map if local business is important to you.

Getting listed on this search is easy thanks to Google Places. It's free to use, so visit **www.google.co.uk/places**. You'll need to be logged into a Google account to use the service. Click the 'Add new business' button. On the next page, United Kingdom should be selected as the country, but select it from the drop-down menu if it isn't. Type your company's phone number into the 'Phone number' box and click 'Find business information'.

If you want to get a lot of local business, it's worth making sure that your company is listed on Google Maps

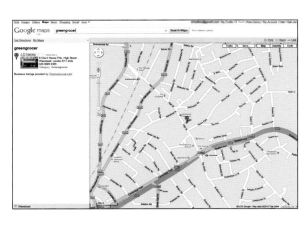

If Google currently holds any information on your company it will be listed, and you can edit an existing entry or add a new listing; if your company doesn't have any current listing, you'll be taken straight to the 'Add a new listing' page. For the purposes of this column, we'll show you how to add a new listing.

You'll be asked to provide some basic information about your business, including its name and location. As you start typing in your business address, the small Google Maps window will zoom into the same location. However, sometimes postcodes can point to the wrong address. You can click the 'Fix incorrect marker location' link and drag the red 'pin' to where your business is located, and click Save Changes. Make sure you get this address correct, or people will be unable to find your company. You can tell Google if your company only operates from one location, or if it will serve customers at their locations. At this point, you can tell Google how far from your location you're willing to travel. You can then set your hours of business and the payment types you take, and add a photo of the premises.

Finally, you can upload a video about your company to YouTube and add additional information, such as whether you have parking or not.

When you're done, click Submit. You'll be taken to a screen to choose a method to verify your listing: by phone, SMS (if you provided a mobile number) or postcard. Select the correct method and click Finish. You'll be sent a PIN by the requested method, which you need to type into the Google Places site. Once this is done, your company will appear on Google Maps.

You can update your company's location manually by dragging the marker around the map

Chapter 9

Top Android tips and tricks

Essential Android apps................. 88

Better browsing in Android 92

Fix common Android problems 94

Make your own Android apps 96

Essential Android apps

There are some fantastic apps available from the Android Market (http://market.android.com). We look at some of our favourites

Chrome to Phone

Ever wished you could transfer something you were reading in your desktop web browser to your phone? Using Chrome to Phone, you can. This app requires you to install the Chrome to Phone Extension for Google Chrome. Log Chrome to Phone into your Google account on your phone and browser, and you can send text and URLs from your browser to your phone. Web pages are opened automatically in your phone's browser, but you can also select text in Chrome and send that. Email addresses pop up in your phone's email client, phone numbers are placed into the dialler and other text is copied to the clipboard.

ESPN Goals

Keeping up with the latest football scores is easy thanks to the ESPN Goals app. It lets you keep track of your team's progress in the league, view upcoming schedules and get live match reports. You can also watch Premier League goals for free. International matches are supported, too, making this app a great resource.

Shazam

Heard a track you like, but don't know the artist? Shazam is the app for you. Press the Listen button and hold the phone up to the external music source, and you'll get a message telling you what the track is. For easy access, there's even a widget you can put on a home screen. It's accurate, even in noisy bars. The free edition lets you tag five tracks a month, and a subscription version lets you tag as many as you like.

Wikidroid

Wikipedia is the ultimate free knowledge source on the internet, and Wikidroid is the ultimate free Android app to access it. When you open it, you are taken to the homepage with the article of the day. From here, you can either browse to a random page or search for a topic of interest. You can add bookmarks for your favourite articles, and the app can even be set as the default for Wikipedia pages, so visiting an article from the browser will launch Wikidroid. The free version is excellent, while the paid-for Wikidroid Plus also lets you save articles for offline viewing.

Sky+

If you're out and about, and you've forgotten to record a programme on your Sky+ or Sky+ HD box, this app can save the day. It lets you view schedules, set recordings and search for programmes – pretty much everything that you can do with a remote control. The only things you can't do are delete recordings, view a current schedule or set up a series link, but this is due to the way the Sky box works.

Skype

After years of having to deal with slightly shoddy applications that were compatible with Skype, the official app is here. It gives you access to all your Skype friends and lets you make VoIP calls. It has the option to become the default dialler for phone numbers, so you can quickly call people using your SkypeOut credit from your phone book.

Google Earth

Google Maps might let you see where you're going and plan routes, but Google Earth allows you to go global. With the help of satellite photography, you can visit places virtually before you get on a plane. Multi-touch support enables you to zoom in and rotate through the display, while a search mode lets you find a place of interest. There's even a 3D mode for some locations, so you can shift your perspective as though you were standing there.

Google Street View

Google Street View is a greatt way to check out an area before you visit it, and it can also help you to plan a route. The updated Street View app in the Market gives you a full-screen view; you can rotate the image and zoom in. Navigation through maps is much easier – just drag the Peg Man to where you want to go, and you'll find yourself at street level in no time.

Google Sky Map

Ever looked up into the night sky and wondered what those stars were called, or where Uranus is? Using GPS information and the compass in your phone, Google Sky Map displays all the major stars and planets in a particular part of the heavens – just hold up your display to the relevant area of the sky to see the results onscreen. There's even a clever search mode; just type in the name of star or

planet, and it will tell you which way to turn to see it. With Sky Map on your phone, you can give Patrick Moore a run for his money.

Google Shopper

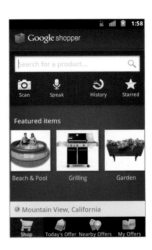

If you're in a shop and want to find out whether you could get a particular product cheaper elsewhere, try Google Shopper. This clever app uses your phone's camera, takes a picture of the item and searches the internet for the latest prices. Its image recognition is unbelievable – it recognised almost all the books and DVDs with which we tried it. If you don't get a match, it will scan barcodes for spot-on product recognition. It's incredibly fast to use and should ensure that you always get the best deal.

Advanced Task Killer

Android's multi-tasking is brilliant, but running loads of apps can slow down your phone. Also, if an app stops responding, it can be difficult to know what to do. This is a clever app that runs all the

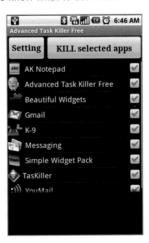

time and can be accessed from the pull-down menu at the top of the screen. Once in it, you can close a specific app or shut down all running applications, thereby freeing up lots of system resources. The latest version will even monitor apps and shut them down after a set period of inactivity. Use this app and your phone will always be silky smooth, and you'll never run short of system resources again.

Compass

Sometimes it's just good to know which way you're heading, or which way to turn in order to face North. Compass turns

▶

your phone's screen into a traditional compass. However, because this is the 21st century, you can also save your favourite places (such as your restaurant) and navigate back to them whenever you like.

Angry Birds
iPhone users have to pay for this highly amusing game, but it's free for Android owners. The aim is to take control of the angry birds and fight the green pigs to get back

your eggs. You must fire a variety of birds at the pigs' fortifications, destroying the pigs as you go. It's brilliant fun and completely addictive.

London Tube Status
If you ever use the tube in London, this app is vital. It connects to the Transport for London website and pulls down the status information. It tells you which lines are running and if there are any delays. Even better, you can select a station and find out when the next tube trains are due. People who make regular journeys can add widgets to the phone's home screen in order to receive updates.

Eurostar trains
This new app lets you book your seat on a Eurostar train from your smartphone. You can search and pay for journeys between London, Paris and Brussels, check in by scanning your phone and save your seating preferences for future trips. Regular travellers can also view their loyalty points.

Twitter
There are plenty of Twitter apps for Android, but few are as good as the official Twitter client. Its clear interface lets you read Tweets, update your status, manage friends and more besides, and all incredibly quickly. It also comes with a widget that lets you view the most recent messages without having to load up the full app. If you have a Twitter account, this is a must-have for your phone.

GPS Alarm
Ever fallen asleep on a train and missed your station? GPS Alarm will ensure you never miss your stop again. After you run it, just select your destination on the map. As soon as you get to where you're going, the alarm sounds and wakes you up. Next time you're on a long commute, use GPS Alarm to be sure of getting to your destination refreshed.

Sky News
The official Sky News app can help you to keep up to date with the latest news, and it's a great example of how Android is garnering mainstream support. It lets you view the top stories, filter by category (such as, showbiz, UK, sport and politics) and keep abreast of what's going on. The video button lets you watch the latest news clips if you prefer video to reading. Finally, the Report button enables you to interact with Sky News and send an image or video from your phone to the newsroom.

Vevo

Vevo's smartphone app allows you to watch more than 25,000 high-quality music videos from 7,500 artists. You can search for songs using your voice, create playlists of your favourite videos and discover what's popular in your area using the Music Map tool.

ColorNote Notepad Notes

There's no better way to stay organised than with ColorNote Notepad Notes. This handy app lets you take notes quickly and efficiently on your phone. It provides standard notes and to-do lists. You can lock notes so they are viewed only when you enter a password. In addition, you can colour-code all the notes in order to quickly group together notes on a similar subject. Notes can also be arranged alphabetically or by time modified, plus you can add timed reminders to help you stay on top of your affairs.

We7 Radio Plus

This app lets you create and listen to your own radio station, based around artists, genres and themes (such as 'air guitar anthems') of your choice. To get started, sign up for a free We7 account, connect your smartphone to a Wi-Fi network and 'charge' it with music (download songs).

IMDb

Whether you want to settle an argument about films or look up an actor you recognise while watching TV, the Internet Movie Database (IMDb) is invaluable. Why bother with the website when you can get it all perfectly formatted for your smartphone's screen? The official IMDb app is a must-have for film fans and gives you everything the site does.

Argos

Following the success of its iPhone app, Argos has launched an Android version that offers the same features. Browse more than 25,000 products, find your nearest branch using the store locator, and check the price and stock of individual items. You can also view all the latest price cuts.

Skyscanner

This app saves you money on air travel by comparing flights from hundreds of airlines around the world. You can quickly see the cheapest days to fly and buy tickets directly through the app, from airlines or travel agents.

Bit-tech Free

Get all the latest computing news from Bit-tech's free Android app (an ad-free version is available for £1.79). You can read in-depth reviews of hardware and software, listen to the team's weekly podcast and chat to other users via the forums and blogs.

Foodspotting

If you're feeling peckish, you can use this app to find something tasty to eat nearby. Rather than listing restaurant reviews, Foodspotting features photos of specific dishes and tells you where you can order them. And when you're enjoying a meal, you can 'nom' it, take a snap and share the details.

Doctor Who: The Mazes of Time

This ambitious game from BBC Worldwide costs £1.49 on the iPhone but is free to download on Android (although you'll need to pay for upgrade packs). Guide the Doctor and Amy through 100 levels of puzzles, facing familiar enemies such as the Daleks and Cybermen.

Blippar

Augmented-reality app Blippar uses your phone's camera to recognise real-world items such as posters, newspaper adverts and food products. The app then overlays the object with games, videos and web links. Cadbury is currently offering Blippar content via its chocolate bars.

Better browsing in Android

Here are five clever ways to boost your web browsing in Android

All versions from Android 2.2 (Froyo) onwards have had support for Adobe Flash, which means you can view all content on the web. This, combined with tabbed browsing and some clever zooming tools, means that the experience of browsing the internet on your Android device closely matches that on a laptop or desktop computer.

INSTALLATION

If you're running Android 2.2 or later, you should install Adobe Flash Player 10 on your handset. Go to the Market, search for Adobe Flash Player and install the application

you find. It integrates automatically with the browser on your device. Now, when you go to a website that has Flash content, such as the BBC iPlayer website, you'll be able to view everything.

Flash content can be processor-intensive for a mobile device, and you may not want to have every bit of Flash content loading by default. This is easy to fix. In your browser, click the Menu button, select More and Settings. Go to 'Enable plug-ins' and change the setting to 'on demand'. Then when you visit a website with Flash content, you'll have to tap it to get it to load.

BOOKMARKS

Adding bookmarks is as easy in Android as it is on a desktop PC. When a page has finished loading, you'll see an icon next to the web page address. Tap this to go to

the Bookmarks page and select 'Add over the thumbnail'. You can get back to this menu by pressing the Menu button and selecting Bookmarks. From here, you can tap a bookmark to open it; a long press lets you edit it, open it in a new window, delete it, add a shortcut to the home screen, and share the address of the bookmark. View most visited websites and browsing history by tapping icons at the top of the page.

HOME PAGE

To set a home page, long-press a bookmark and choose the option, or go to Settings and select 'Set home page'. Type in the address or select 'Use current page'. There's no dedicated Home button in Android, but the first time you start the browser, and every time you open a new browser window, you're taken to your home page.

NEW WINDOWS

Just as you can have multiple tabs in a desktop browser, you can have multiple windows in Android. To open a new window, press Menu and then New Window. You can add a new window and view existing windows by pressing Menu, Windows. Tap a window to jump to it or press the X to shut it down. If you close all the open windows, a new one is opened up with your home page.

ZOOMING AND TEXT

You can zoom in to a web page in three ways. First, you can pinch on the screen, secondly, you can touch the screen and use the magnifying glasses, and finally, you can double-tap an area you want to view; this has the added advantage of reformatting text to fit the new zoom, making it easier to read.

It's possible to control all these options in Settings, where you can set the text size, the default zoom level and whether pages should be formatted automatically to fit the screen.

Fix common Android problems

Simple solutions to fixing the most common Android problems

Android's not perfect, and there will be times when it goes wrong. Most of the problems you'll have will be related to third-party apps rather than Android itself, but we have seen system components go wrong, such as the Android Market. That said, you may never encounter a problem – and even if you do, most issues can be fixed easily.

FIXING AN APP
With thousands of apps available for Android, and countless handsets to run them, you're bound to encounter some problems with apps. Generally, we've found that big-name apps such as Skype and Facebook work well; you're far more likely to have problems with games and apps for niche interests. Below are a couple of things you can try to get an app running again.

Uninstalling updates
Open up the Android Market and browse to your apps. Find the offending app and see if there's an option to uninstall updates. If there is, select this and your app will be rolled back to the previous version. If this works, try applying the update again. This is useful with broken system apps such as Google Maps and Gmail, which can't be uninstalled.

Some system apps can have updates uninstalled only via Settings, Applications, Manage Applications, All Applications. Tap the app in question and select 'Uninstall updates'.

Uninstalling and then reinstalling an app
If an app is broken, your best bet is to uninstall and reinstall it. Go to the Market and select My Apps. Find the troublesome app and select Uninstall. Select it again and reinstall it. That should fix it. Sadly, this won't work for system apps, which can't be uninstalled.

CLEARING DATA
Sometimes clearing data is the only way to fix a problem. Go to Settings, Applications, Manage applications. Tap the app you're interested in and select 'Force stop' to kill it. Then select 'Clear cache' and 'Clear data'. If this works, you may need to re-enter login details for some apps. Be careful, as this will wipe an application's data from your phone – you'll need to make sure that you've made a back-up beforehand.

RESETTING YOUR PHONE
If none of the above works (or your problem is with a system app or Android itself), then Safe mode or a factory reset ought to solve your problems. Before a reset, make sure any data on your phone is stored safely somewhere. As long as you were syncing online with a Gmail account, your contacts, email and calendar appointments will be backed up and your apps can be downloaded from the Market. Just check that you've backed up any application data, either inside an application or using a program such as MyBackup Pro.

TOP ANDROID TIPS AND TRICKS

Using safe mode

Getting into Safe mode depends on your handset, so it's best to Google the exact manufacturer and model plus the words 'safe mode' to find out the exact instructions. In general, though, you have to turn off the phone and remove the battery, and wait for at least two minutes before replacing it. Press and hold the Menu button, then press the Power button. Hold down the Menu button until the phone has started, and you should see the words 'Safe mode' onscreen. Power down the phone, take the battery out and wait for two minutes before replacing it, then restart the phone.

Factory reset

For a basic clean sheet, you'll want to 'factory reset' your phone. Go to Settings, Privacy (or Storage, where some HTC phones have this setting). Make sure 'Back up my data' and 'Automatic restore' are selected; this will restore your phone when it restarts. Then select 'Factory data reset'. When your phone restarts, touch the Android logo and follow the wizard. Enter the same primary Google account you were using before, and your phone will restore your wallpaper and settings and attempt to download all your apps from the Android Market. You may, however, need to upgrade to the latest version.

Making a complete reset

If you're still having problems, the best thing to do is wipe everything completely. Go to Settings, Storage and select 'Unmount SD card', then select 'Erase SD card' to wipe it. Then go to Settings, Applications, Manage Applications and tap All. Select each one in turn and, where available, tap 'Force stop', 'Clear data' and 'Clear cache'. This will wipe all your phone's stored settings.

Finally, go to Settings, Privacy (or Storage, where some HTC phones have this setting). Make sure 'Back up my data' and 'Automatic restore' are not selected to prevent your phone restoring bad data when it restarts. Select 'Factory data reset'. When your phone starts, you'll have to reinstall everything manually and configure your accounts again, but everything else should go back to normal.

ANDROID MARKET

For reasons unknown, the Android Market will often fail because it doesn't like the network connection you're using. We've suffered most of our problems when connected over a Wi-Fi network, so try disabling wireless and connecting using 3G. If that's not an option, try disconnecting and reconnecting the wireless, then attempt your download again. Sometimes it's the wireless network you're on that causes the problems. For example, if you're on a corporate network it may be firewalled to prevent the downloads working or letting Google Talk work.

Clear application data

Sometimes, to thoroughly fix a problem with Android Market, you need to wipe some application data and start afresh. To do this go to the Settings, Applications menu and click 'All applications'. To clear data of an application, select it and click 'Force stop' (not strictly necessary, but worth doing) and click 'Clear data'. Follow this procedure for Download Manager, Market and Market Updater. For Market, you may also want to click Uninstall Updates, if the option is available.

Make your own Android apps

It sounds daunting, but writing an Android app is easy. Here's how...

Writing applications for mobile devices has traditionally demanded a lot of effort. Extras, such as adaptor cables and custom hardware, have often been required, too. Only a couple of years ago, you might have needed to spend at least a few hundred pounds on software and extras before you could write a single line of code. And even once you had the tools, setting yourself up for mobile device development was a tortuous nightmare of configuration.

Today, however, it's easy to develop an app for an Android phone or tablet – so simple that you don't need to write any code. In fact, you don't even need an Android device to get started.

In this chapter, we'll take a look at the challenges of programming for mobile platforms (and embedded devices, which are fundamentally very similar), and we'll show you how to get your very own mobile app running on an Android smartphone.

Cross-compilation

Embedded and mobile devices are generally programmed in the same languages as desktop programming – primarily C and C++. But you can't write a program in one of those languages on a PC and then run it on another device. That's because these devices use processor hardware and architectures that are completely unlike those of a PC. These processors understand different machine instructions, so you can't compile your mobile application using a standard desktop development environment. You need to use a process called cross-compiling – generating code on one system to run on another.

Cross-compilation brings problems. In the real world, you'll never write bug-free code first time round. Code is usually developed through a fairly tight cycle: you compile your program, run it to see what the bugs and errors are, tweak the code, recompile it and try again. Even professional developers tend to use this trial-and-error approach, sometimes recompiling and running their code dozens of times an hour.

With cross-compilation, this isn't possible: the PC on which you're developing doesn't understand the code it's producing, because it's being compiled for another hardware platform. So to test your application you need to compile it, then transfer the resulting code to the external device for testing. Often this entails rebooting or resetting the device, so a process that takes a couple of seconds when developing a standard local PC application turns into something that takes minutes or more.

To make matters worse, you can't use traditional runtime debugging tools, such as variable watchers and breakpoints, to keep track of what's happening as your code executes, which makes the process of debugging more difficult.

Happily, there's a more convenient way to test cross-compiled code: using emulation. Rather than having to upload the code to an external device every time you want to test it, you can 'upload' it to an emulated version of that hardware, which is actually running on your development PC. This emulator can understand and run the code produced by your cross-compiler.

Emulators are highly complex pieces of software; traditionally, they've been expensive both to produce and buy. But thanks to the power of open-source software, you can install an Android emulator suitable for testing cross-compiled code without reaching for your credit card.

Enter the App Inventor

The existence of a free Android emulator is a big help when it comes to creating Android applications. But if you want to write heavyweight, commercial-quality software, you'll still need a degree of proficiency in programming in Java, which is the 'native' language for Android devices. (In fact, applications run within a semi-proprietary virtual machine called Dalvik, which is similar to Java but a little more memory-efficient.)

If you aren't familiar with Java, however – or indeed with programming in general – all is not lost. Thanks to Google's clever App Inventor, you don't need to be a programming expert to produce your own Android applications. In this free, web-based development environment, you can create applications graphically by dragging and dropping functional building blocks.

At first sight App Inventor may look like a toy, but it allows you to build some surprisingly sophisticated software. It also allows you to access the phone's hardware, so you can create applications that make use of geolocation information, connect to databases, access social networks such as Twitter, and interact with websites. You don't even need an Android device to get started: the emulator gives you a full Android-based phone environment, complete with graphical user interface and emulated hardware buttons.

Anatomy of App Inventor

There are three sections to App Inventor. First there's the Designer, where you create your graphical user interface (GUI), laying out all the necessary buttons, tickboxes and GUI furniture for your user. This section of App Inventor runs in your browser as a web application.

Next is the Blocks Editor, a Java application that runs locally on your PC. This is where you do your 'programming', dragging logical blocks around and connecting them to elements of your GUI to respond to inputs from the user.

Finally, there's the all-important emulator. This is a native Windows application, which you'll need to install as part of the initial setup process. The setup is a little fiddly, but it mainly involves making sure your PC's Java setup is configured correctly. To do this, you'll need to

go to http://appinventor.googlelabs.com and follow the steps there.

You start by visiting a test page, which will tell you if your Java Virtual Machine installation is the latest version. If not, it will give you a helpful download link; like everything else in App Inventor, the Java download is free. You then click a Java app link to check the Web Start Launcher is up and running. This is the helper application that allows Java apps to download and run when you click a website link.

The Android emulator is a complete emulation of a real Android phone

Once Java is sorted, you can download the App Inventor installer package, the primary purpose of which is to install the emulator back-end. Once this is done, sign into your Google or Gmail account, then head to http://appinventor.googlelabs.com and the Designer web app will appear in your browser.

Your first app

The workshop on the following pages will guide you through the necessary steps to create your first application; but before diving into that, it's fun to spend a bit of time experimenting in the Designer.

To get started, click New at the top left of the Designer window, enter a name for your test app and hit Enter. The main design interface will appear, with a blank canvas in the middle representing your phone's screen, and a raft of GUI components on the left begging to be played with.

To add a GUI component to your application, drag it onto the phone's screen, then play with its settings on the right. For instance, you can brighten up your application's front-end by dragging an Image component over. Drop it on the screen, then click the Add button under Media on the right, and browse for an image to place within the GUI.

Drag across a ListPicker and, as the name suggests, you'll get a GUI element that the user can tap on to ▶

choose from a list of elements. Once it's in place, you can populate it by typing comma-separated list entries into the ElementsFromString box on the right – for example, you might type 'Red,Green,Blue'.

You've now created an Android app, which you can run either on the emulator or your phone. It won't do anything useful, but it's in a runnable state. If you don't believe us, see for yourself: click the button at the top right of the Designer window labelled Open the Blocks Editor. When the Blocks Editor opens, ignore the main interface for now, and click New Emulator at the top right. The emulator can take a minute or two to start, and once the emulator itself is running it needs to boot up the Android OS, which again can take a little time. Once it's up and running you'll see a full emulation of an Android phone in front of you, complete with buttons.

Now, back in the Blocks Editor, hit Connect to Device and select the only option: 'emulator-5554'. Switch back to the emulator, wait another minute or so, and hey presto – your GUI will appear.

Getting to this point may have been slow, but from now on all changes you make to your app, in either the Designer or Blocks Editor, will be automatically compiled and uploaded to the emulator. This will make ongoing development and testing extremely easy.

Making it go
We started our demonstration application by placing interface elements, which is normal: in modern application design, whether mobile or desktop, the first step is almost always to create your GUI. Only then do you write your functioning program code, defining what happens when the user presses a button or chooses an option.

This is known as an event-driven programming model: almost all modern apps present the user with a graphical interface when they start up, but do nothing further until the user interacts with that interface. When the user does click something, the app generates an event, which then calls the part of the program you've written to deal with that particular scenario.

In App Inventor, you create this code in the Blocks Designer. Our workshop (opposite) shows you how to assemble some basic functions via the Blocks Editor, so you can get a feel for it.

Limitations
App Inventor is more powerful than you might expect, though it's worth knowing that its block-based approach isn't quite as flexible as a traditional text editor-based development environment.

The real limitation is that once you've produced your incredible-looking app, there's no way to make your fortune from it, since it can't be published on the Android Market. This is a technical limitation, rather than a policy decision on Google's part, though, and there's every chance it's a situation that will change in the near future.

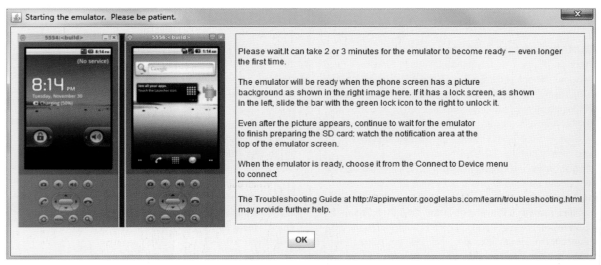

If the emulator doesn't seem to be working, be patient; it's a complex piece of software and it takes a while to start up

Making an Android app with App Inventor

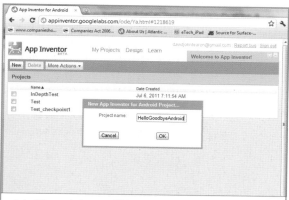

1 In this workshop, we'll build a simple app that switches between two images when the user clicks a button. Follow the directions on pages 97-98 to get the Designer, Blocks Editor and emulator up and running. Then, in the Designer, click New Project, give it a suitable name – we've gone with 'HelloGoodbyeAndroid' – and click OK.

2 In the main Designer window, drag a Button element onto the phone screen in the middle of the display; then add an Image element. Under Properties, set the text for Button1 to 'Goodbye!'. You'll see other properties are available here, too: you can change the font, text size and style if you like.

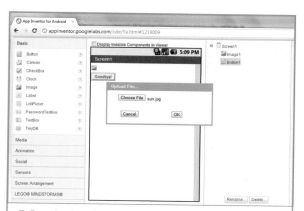

3 Download our images from www.pcpro.co.uk/links/appinventor. Unzip the file and inside you'll find a pair of files, named sun.jpg and moon.jpg. Save them somewhere convenient, then click Add under the Media heading toward the bottom right of the screen. Browse to each image in turn, clicking OK to upload it.

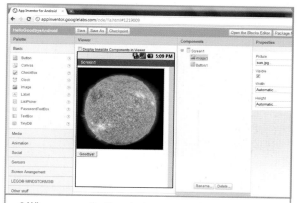

4 When our application starts, we want the image of the sun to be displayed by default. To achieve this, we simply load the file into our Image element. In the Designer, click the Image1 element, then, in the Properties pane to the right, click the Picture text area. Select sun.jpg and hit OK to place the image.

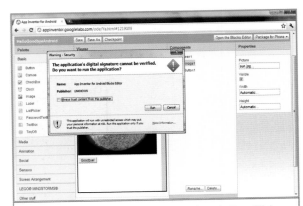

5 Next we want to set the behaviour of our button. Click 'Open the Blocks Editor' at the top right of the Designer window and you'll be prompted to download the module. Run it, if it doesn't launch automatically. You'll see a security warning, but it's safe to run the app. (Hopefully, a future version will remove this unhelpful warning.)

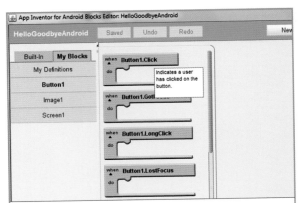

6 When the Blocks Editor starts, click the My Blocks tab, then click Button1. You'll see a selection of blocks that can be used to set behaviours relating to this button. Drag the topmost block – labelled 'Button1.click' – onto the main area of the window. Now click Image1, and drag out the block labelled 'set Image1.Picture to'.

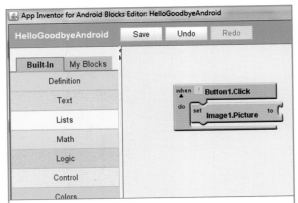

7 Drag 'set Image1.Picture to' into the middle of the Button1.click element. It will snap into place: compatible blocks fit together like jigsaw pieces. Now, the action specified by the inner block will be triggered whenever the event specified by the outer block happens – in this case, when the button is clicked.

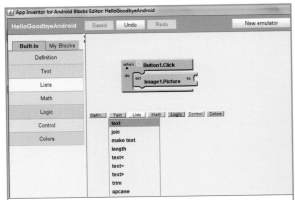

8 Left-click on an empty part of the main window. You'll see a series of buttons appear. Left-click the one marked 'Text' to open a submenu, and from this submenu again select the entry 'text'. You'll see a new block appear labelled 'text'. Click on the large text on this block to edit it: set it to 'moon.jpg'.

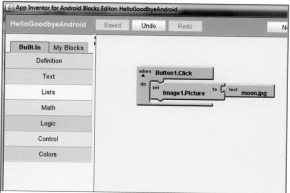

9 Drag the text block you just created and connect it to the end of the Image1.Picture element. Our event handler is complete. If you wanted, you could slot in additional actions within the Click event – before or after this one – but these three blocks are all we need to change the photo when the user clicks the 'Goodbye!' button.

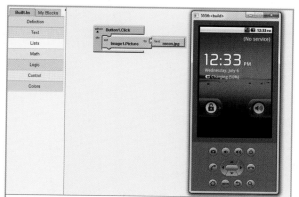

10 The next stage is to test our app. To do this, click New Emulator in the Blocks Editor. Heed the warning that it can take a few minutes to start up: it really can, and once the emulated phone appears, the Android OS also has to boot. Eventually, though, a virtual Android phone will appear on your screen.

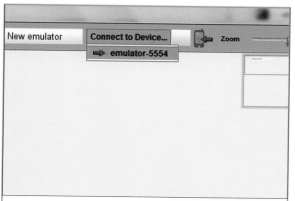

11 Once the emulator is up and running, click Connect to Device and select 'emulator-5554'. This is all you need to do for the app to be uploaded into the emulated phone and start executing. Once App Inventor is connected to the emulator, any changes you make to the app are automatically uploaded.

12 Using the mouse, swipe the unlock icon across the emulated Android screen to unlock the 'phone'. You should see our application already running, showing the default picture of the sun. Click the 'Goodbye!' button with the mouse – simulating a finger press – and the image will change to the moon.

Chapter 10

Android tablets tested

How we tested the tablets 104

Acer Iconia Tab A500 105

HTC Flyer 106

Asus Eee Pad Transformer 108

Samsung Galaxy Tab 10.1 110

LG Optimus Pad 3D 112

Motorola Xoom 114

Advent Vega 115

Dell Streak 115

Creative Zii0 7in 115

ViewSonic ViewPad 10s 115

How we tested the tablets

With different versions of Androids, it's impossible to develop system-level benchmarks that run on every tablet. However, there are still plenty of parameters that can be measured, which give substance to our appraisals.

Browser speed
Almost all popular commercial websites rely on JavaScript to render pages, and all tablet browsers support JavaScript. Measuring JavaScript performance gives us an idea of the

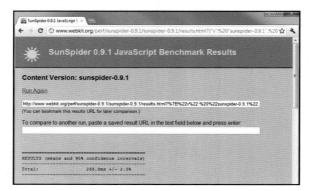

quality of the browsing experience and how quickly pages render. We did this by running the SunSpider 0.9.1 test (http://bit.ly/sunspidertest) in the tablet's native browser, which gave a result in milliseconds (ms). We also backed this up with a real-world test, clearing the browser cache, and then timing how long it takes to load the full BBC homepage over a fast Wi-Fi connection.

Battery life
To measure a tablet's battery life, we shut off wireless connections and played a 320 x 240-pixel podcast video on loop until the battery ran out.

Screen brightness
For this test, we turned the brightness up, then used a colorimeter to measure the luminance of pure white and black screens to gauge the maximum brightness, the black point and the contrast ratio.

Camera
We tested the camera's photo and video quality using standard indoor, low-light and outdoor scenarios.

Acer Iconia Tab A500

PRICE From £460 **SIZE** 10.1in **SUPPLIER** www.insight.com

A solid Android tablet, but others offer better quality for this kind of money

As soon as you pick up the Acer Iconia Tab A500, it's obvious that plenty of attention has been lavished on the design. The brushed-aluminium rear panel wraps neatly around the long edges of the tablet. Build quality is excellent, the volume and lock buttons on the top edge are finished in eye-catching chrome, and the capacitive glass screen resists smudges and smears nicely.

Acer has done a fine job on Android integration, too. Where the Motorola Xoom has a tendency to judder, the A500 always feels smooth and responsive. It loaded the BBC homepage in five seconds, completed the SunSpider JavaScript benchmark in 1,908ms and gained 1,887 points in Quadrant – all scores that put its performance up with the best in this chapter. That's hardly surprising given that it has the same dual-core 1GHz Nvidia Tegra processor as six of its rivals.

Bright and beautiful

The screen is reasonably bright – we measured a maximum of 312cd/m² – with good contrast. The Acer lasted 10hrs 1min in our battery test; connectivity is fine, too, with micro-USB and HDMI ports, plus a full-sized USB socket in the right-hand corner. A 3G option (the A501) is available for £76 more, and Acer bundles the A500 with a number of media-streaming applications and three HD games: Let's Golf 2, Heroes of Sparta and Need For Speed Shift.

It's a decent package, but the A500 falls short in a couple of key areas. The first is its weight. This isn't something you notice at first, and 756g doesn't seem too concerning on paper, but after a few minutes reading a book, playing a game or watching a video, the corners start digging uncomfortably into your palms.

Another reason is the fixed storage – you can't yet add more, either via the USB port or the microSD slot. A future update should fix

the issue, but there's no indication as to when this might happen. Finally, the price isn't that enticing either.

If it's an Android 3 (Honeycomb) tablet you're after, the Asus Eee Pad Transformer (see p108) is cheaper, lighter, has a better screen and its memory expansion works. We'd look very closely at Asus' tablet before we'd even consider the Acer Iconia Tab A500.

OVERALL ★★★★★★

PERFORMANCE ★★★★★★
BATTERY LIFE ★★★★★★
FEATURES & DESIGN ★★★★★★
VALUE FOR MONEY ★★★★★★

HTC Flyer

PRICE From £385.99, Wi-Fi only; £414.99, 3G **SIZE** 7in **SUPPLIER** www.amazon.co.uk

A lovely design, but silly pricing makes it difficult to recommend

HTC's Sense skin for Android is a familiar sight on its smartphones, but it's now made its way onto the firm's debut tablet. That's something of a controversial move on the Flyer, because it sits on top of Android 2.3 (Gingerbread), the latest smartphone version of the operating system – not the tablet-specific Android 3, which is installed on other tablets we tested.

You might think that would be a problem on a tablet's larger 7in 1,024 x 600 screen, but in fact we rather enjoyed using the Flyer's enhanced phone-based interface. Its attractive custom widgets suit the dimensions of the screen much better than the standard-issue ones on the Samsung Galaxy Tab 10.1 (see p110). And many of the HTC apps included as standard – including the image gallery, email and calendar – have been enhanced so they're more space-efficient when you tilt the tablet into landscape mode.

Everything from menus to the keyboard responds promptly and smoothly, and web page panning and zooming effects flow better than on the stuttering Samsung Galaxy Tab 10.1 or the cheap Creative Zii0 7in. There are also benefits to running Android 2.3: many apps that fail to run on Android 3 (Honeycomb) work without a hitch on the Flyer.

HTC has followed Apple's lead in building its tablet from a curvaceous slab of slender aluminium and, coupled with the Gorilla Glass on the front, it feels lovely to hold. We're not so keen on the wide white-plastic strips on the rear – one of which can be removed to reveal the microSD and SIM card slots – but they do ensure the aluminium finish doesn't scratch easily when you put it down.

Unique feature

The fantastic design extends to the Flyer's most unusual feature. In the box, along with a white slip case, you'll find a weighty aluminium stylus, which allows you not only to scrawl notes and doodles in the HTC Notepad app, but also to highlight text and make page annotations in the supplied eBook reader. With apps that don't support the pen, you can simply tap the screen to take a screenshot, then annotate it in the Notepad app and upload the results to Evernote.

With good performance in all our tests and a nice, bright screen, the HTC Flyer might have scored top marks, despite what some would call a rather backwards-looking approach, but it's undermined by a few silly mistakes. The stylus is wonderful, but there's nowhere to stow it in the body of the tablet; you're forced to use the loop on the slip case, which is a clumsy solution. Much worse is the dreadful 5-megapixel camera, which produces over-compressed stills and smeary video.

Battery life is a mediocre 8hrs 4mins, but by far the biggest issue is the price, which at £385.99 for a 7in Wi-Fi-only tablet and £414.99 for the 3G version is simply too high. There are much cheaper alternatives, and only a serious rethink on pricing can see the Flyer compete for value.

OVERALL ★★★★★★

PERFORMANCE ★★★★★★
BATTERY LIFE ★★★★★★
FEATURES & DESIGN ★★★★★★
VALUE FOR MONEY ★★★★★★

Asus Eee Pad Transformer

PRICE From £342.45, Wi-Fi only; £417.97, with keyboard dock **SIZE 10.1**in **SUPPLIER** www.amazon.co.uk

A cracking tablet with top performance and a very tempting price

No other tablet in this chapter is quite like the Asus Eee Pad Transformer. Half laptop, half tablet, it combines the joys of Android 3 (Honeycomb) with the typing power and pointing precision of a keyboard and touchpad. It's an intriguing proposition, and one that makes the Transformer the most flexible of all the tablets in this chapter.

The device comes in two halves. The tablet part can be used like an ordinary tablet, but it can also be employed as a pseudo netbook: clip it into the hinge of the optional keyboard base (£50) whenever the fancy takes you.

The keyboard and touchpad don't add that much to the usability of Android 3, though, despite support for multitouch gestures. It's an operating system designed for

touch, and we soon grew tired of continually reaching over to tap onscreen icons and buttons, effectively ignoring the presence of the touchpad.

But the base is about more than only the keyboard and touchpad. It also adds a pair of USB ports and an SD card slot for storage expansion and file transfer, plus an extra battery. The latter keeps the battery in the tablet topped up when connected, extending its battery life from a middling 8hrs 37mins to 15hrs 43mins.

Without the keyboard dock, the Transformer still impresses. The price is reasonable: at £379 for the 16GB version it's the cheapest of all the Android 3 tablets, and it doesn't cut corners. The superb display features an IPS

panel, like that of the iPad, which brings wide viewing angles and fantastic colour reproduction. Brightness is a little down on the best at 326cd/m², but the contrast ratio of 758:1 makes up for that, lending video clips and pictures a real solidity and punch.

Connectivity is second to none. As well as the base's two USB ports and SD card slot, the Eee Pad itself sports a mini-HDMI port, plus a working microSD expansion slot (unlike the Motorola Xoom on p114, whose non-working slot was still awaiting a fix at the time of writing). That means you can boost the 16GB of storage to 32GB for around £15 or to 48GB for around £50.

Performance from the dual-core 1GHz Nvidia Tegra 2 processor was great, too. In our tests, the Transformer loaded the BBC homepage in around five seconds, completed the SunSpider JavaScript test in 2,027ms, and in the Android-specific Quadrant test it achieved 2,041 points – all results that put the Eee Pad near the top of the tree.

There are a few blots on this tablet's copybook, though. There's currently no 3G option, which limits its appeal. The camera produces above average, but hardly exceptional, stills, and 720p video records at a slow 8fps, a problem that should be resolved in a future update. The battery life isn't wonderful without the keyboard base, and the Android Market isn't yet overflowing with tablet-specific apps.

But look past its quirks and the Eee Pad Transformer is one of the best Android tablets here.

OVERALL ★★★★★

PERFORMANCE ★★★★★
BATTERY LIFE ★★★★★
FEATURES & DESIGN ★★★★★
VALUE FOR MONEY ★★★★★

Samsung Galaxy Tab 10.1

PRICE From £399 (£479 inc VAT) **SIZE** 10.1in **SUPPLIER** www.amazon.co.uk

There's a lot to like about this great-looking tablet

It's not hard to see why Apple put so much effort into its legal campaign against the Samsang Galaxy Tab 10.1. It looks eerily, insolently similar to an iPad 2 – and it probably doesn't help that its various capacities and 3G configurations are priced to precisely match Apple's corresponding models.

Apple is right to be worried, because the Galaxy Tab 10.1 has a lot going for it. The looks have been updated since Samsung first demonstrated the device in February 2011, but it's still lighter than the iPad 2 at 565g, and a fraction of a millimetre thinner. The plastic back isn't quite as bulletproof as Apple's metal casing, but like the Asus Eee Pad Transformer it feels sturdy and warm to the touch. The screen is a delight too – a multitouch 1,200 x 800 LCD panel giving more screen space than the iPad 2 and a sharper dot pitch. Based on Samsung's Super PLS technology – the company's own take on IPS – it's as bright and colourful as you could ask for, offering excellent viewing angles and an arresting maximum brightness of 492cd/m2 (brighter than Apple's display), with a punchy contrast ratio of 600:1. The only downside is that, predictably, the widescreen format feels slightly unwieldy in portrait orientation.

Internally, the Galaxy Tab 10.1 is based on a 1GHz Nvidia Tegra 2 dual-core processor, again matching the Asus Transformer. It was no surprise, therefore, to see the SunSpider JavaScript benchmark complete in a very similar 2.4 seconds. The BBC homepage opened in 5.6 seconds, and in the Android-only Quadrant benchmark the Galaxy Tab scored 2,200, again a typical score for a high-end tablet.

In practice, this makes Android 3 (Honeycomb) a snappy experience. The scrolling and rotating animations appear slightly choppy compared to the iPad 2, and when you swipe to scroll up or down a page there's a tiny delay before the movement registers. But these are general Android

niggles, and they're easy to live with. Overall, the apps and front-end are as responsive as you could ask for.

Samsung has also overlaid its TouchWiz 4.0 customisations onto the regular Android interface. These include 'live panels' – large informational widgets for your home screens – and a Mini Apps Tray along the bottom of the home screen.

A showy 'tilt to zoom' feature has also been added to the browser and various interface elements have been spruced up with a clean black-on-white look. These changes aren't too intrusive, but they add little to the experience. Potentially more useful is the preinstalled copy of Polaris Office, plus some bespoke Samsung apps. These include the Social Hub, which combines your social network services into a single interface, and the Music Hub, an integrated music store powered by the 7digital service.

Smooth operator

Many popular video formats can be played out of the box, and there's support for Windows 7's built-in transcoding capabilities to help with movie files in the wrong format. We also found that 720p YouTube videos played without a hiccup, as did standard-definition content from the BBC iPlayer mobile app – though high-definition streams were unwatchable.

For shooting your own video, the rear-facing camera captures sharp 720p footage, but it's a little grainy. Stills look better: the rear autofocus camera takes 3.2-megapixel stills with crisp detail and good, realistic colour even in lowish light – and there's an LED flash to help out if things get too dark. The front-facing camera is just as sharp, but uses a smaller 2-megapixel sensor and a fixed focal length.

Inevitably, we've a few gripes about the hardware. The biggest disappointment is battery life: in our continuous video test, the Galaxy Tab 10.1 managed just 7hrs 18min of

playback off a full charge – 80 minutes less than the Asus Eee Pad Transformer (see p108).

It's annoying, too, that the only regular connector is a 3.5mm headphone socket (plus a SIM slot on the 3G version). Otherwise, all power and data goes through a proprietary 30-pin socket. If you want to hook up an external display, you'll need the external HDMI adaptor, available for around £20 online. There's no microSD slot either, so if you want extra storage, you'll need the similarly priced SD or USB 2 adaptor.

Overall, the Samsung Galaxy Tab 10.1 is a hugely likeable device. With its slick performance, lightweight chassis and excellent screen and speakers, it captures the instinctive, tactile appeal of the iPad better than any Android rival we've seen. It's simply the best Android tablet we've tested.

OVERALL ★★★★★★

PERFORMANCE ★★★★★★
BATTERY LIFE ★★★★★★
FEATURES & DESIGN ★★★★★★
VALUE FOR MONEY ★★★★★★

LG Optimus Pad 3D

PRICE From £750 **SIZE** 7in or 10in **SUPPLIER** www.amazon.co.uk

A great-performing, if very expensive, tablet that also offers 3D

LG looks to be coming to the tablet party pretty late with the Optimus Pad (or the LG V900, going by the packaging), and so has a couple of tricks up its sleeve with which to woo potential customers. Its first unusual feature is its size – with its 8.9in 1,280 x 768 screen, the Optimus Pad sits entirely on its own, with every other manufacturer on the market producing either 7in or 10in models at the moment.

For our money, it's a comfortable compromise between the two sizes, but it's not without its problems. On the plus side, it's a little more portable than most 10in tablets, and thus better suited to reading on the go. It's more comfortable for browsing the web than a 7in tablet, too. The disappointments start with the thickness and weight. At 18mm its girth is more than double that of the iPad 2 and Galaxy Tab (see p110), and at 620g it's heavier than both.

We're not keen on the extra-wide aspect ratio display, either, which makes it even less conducive to using in portrait mode than the 1,280 x 800 screen on models such as the Asus Eee Pad Transformer (see p108). Finally, the tighter pixel pitch also means buttons and onscreen options are generally fiddlier to use too.

The other prong to LG's unusual approach is 3D, and alas it's just as hit-and-miss. It has a pair of cameras on its rear – two 5-megapixel digital cameras – which allow the tablet to shoot video in stereoscopic 3D at 720p.

However, the Optimus Pad has a standard TFT screen, so to view this footage you either have to hook the tablet up to a proper 3D-enabled TV via the tablet's HDMI output, or don the red and blue anaglyph glasses provided in the box, and prepare for 1980s-style 3D.

If that wasn't bad enough, the software integration is very light. To shoot, browse and play 3D footage on the tablet itself, you have to use separate apps to the standard Android 3 (Honeycomb) ones, and within these there are no options to directly upload the footage to YouTube and share it with friends. You have to use the standard Honeycomb app for that.

Solid performer

Aside from the disappointing headline features, though, the LG Optimus Pad is a perfectly solid tablet. It appears to be well made – the soft plastic rear doesn't creak or bend, and the finish makes it grippy and comfortable to hold. The display itself is bright and clear – we measured it at an iPad 2-beating maximum brightness of 398cd/m² and a sound 622:1 contrast ratio.

Inside the chassis, the Optimus is powered by the same dual-core, 1GHz Nvidia Tegra 2 technology that all other Android 3 tablets have used so far, and the figures show it's just as nippy. In the SunSpider JavaScript benchmark, the LG gained a result of 1,994ms, loading the BBC homepage in an average time of six seconds over a fast Wi-Fi connection, and achieved 1,923 points in the Android Quadrant benchmark. Again, all pretty standard results.

Battery life is good: in our looping low-resolution video test, the Optimus lasted a smidgeon over nine hours – significantly short of the Motorola Xoom (see p114), but longer than both the Samsung Galaxy Tab 10.1 (see p110) and the Asus Eee Pad Transformer (see p108).

Life through a lens

The 5-megapixel camera, used in 2D mode, produces good quality shots – as good as any we've seen from a tablet so far (although it does have a tendency to underexpose a touch), and it records smooth, crisp and detailed 1080p video.

Under a small plastic panel at the rear lurks a slot for a SIM card, allowing you to untether the tablet from your Wi-Fi network and use it anywhere you can get a mobile phone signal. And although there's only one model available in the UK right now, this has a decent 32GB of storage onboard.

So overall, despite a few foibles, the LG Optimus Pad 3D is a solid product, with sound performance, good battery life and a decent camera. What isn't quite so attractive is the high price.

OVERALL ★★★★★★
PERFORMANCE ★★★★★★
BATTERY LIFE ★★★★★★
FEATURES & DESIGN ★★★★★★
VALUE FOR MONEY ★★★★★★

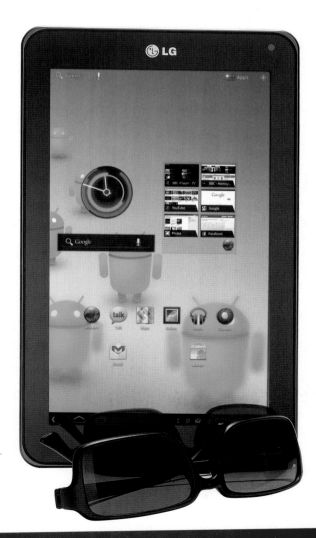

Motorola Xoom

PRICE From £399.99 **SIZE** 10.1in **SUPPLIER** www.play.com

For the price, we'd expect a more refined user experience

The Motorola Xoom was the first Android 3 (Honeycomb) tablet to appear back at the start of 2011, but despite the head start it feels no more polished than more recently launched rivals. In fact, there are an awful lot more ragged edges than you'll find in the Asus Eee Pad Transformer (see p108), for example.

The microSD slot doesn't yet work so you can't expand the memory (although an update is promised), and in use the Motorola Xoom doesn't feel quite as responsive and slick as its rivals. User interface animations, for example, aren't as smooth as they are on the Eee Pad.

Impressive hardware

That's a shame, since the hardware inside is perfectly capable. As with the other Android 3 tablets in this chapter, there's a dual-core Nvidia Tegra 2 processor under the hood, backed up with 1GB of RAM, and the 32GB of internal storage provides plenty of room for apps, music and video. There's a pair of cameras: a 5-megapixel unit with a dual-LED flash on the rear, capable of shooting 720p video, and a 2-megapixel one on the front for video calls. There's a 3G option available for an extra £110 as well.

The cameras are middling in quality, but the 10in 1,366 x 768 screen is one of the best. With our colorimeter, we measured its screen at 358cd/m², which puts it in the top third for brightness this month, and the contrast ratio of 1,377:1 is superb. Where it lags behind a little is in the vibrancy of its colours: it looks a little washed out when sat next to the Asus Eee Pad Transformer. It's no deal-breaker, though.

Battery life is the best of any of the tablets we tested, too, lasting an impressive 12hrs 49mins in our looping video test. And build quality is simply gorgeous, with a subtly curved rear panel decked out in cool anodised aluminium and high-quality soft-touch plastic. As an object, the Motorola Xoom comes closer than any other tablet to rivalling the sheer desirability of the Apple iPad 2.

It may be a superb piece of hardware, but it falls between two stools. It's neither polished enough in all areas to rival the iPad, nor cheap enough to provide a low-cost alternative, as the Asus Eee Pad Transformer does.

OVERALL ★★★★☆

PERFORMANCE ★★★★★
BATTERY LIFE ★★★★★
FEATURES & DESIGN ★★★★☆
VALUE FOR MONEY ★★★☆☆

Four Android 2.2 (Froyo) tablets

Advent Vega

PRICE From £199.99
OVERALL ★★★★☆

The Vega has been around for some time now, and its low price has made it a popular choice. It's easy to see why: inside is a dual-core 1GHz Nvidia Tegra 2 CPU, backed by 512GB of RAM and battery life isn't bad either. Its software isn't as cutting edge. It runs a version of Android 2.2 that looks ugly, and there's no access to the Android Market. Its main problem, though, is an appalling screen: at 235cd/m² it's very dim, and vertical viewing angles are dreadful.

It's a good tablet for hacking, and you can even shoehorn Android 3 on to it, but that can't persuade us it's worth putting up with such a horrid screen.

Creative Zii0 7in

PRICE From £150
OVERALL ★★★☆☆

The Zii0's low price means that the odd compromise has been made, but if you can cope with this it's worth considering.

The screen is resistive, but it's bright and responsive. That, coupled with its small size and apt-X wireless audio codec, makes it a candidate for a do-it-all music, video and reader device.

What it can't offer is a simple way to add apps: it runs a Creative-modified version of Android 2.2 that doesn't have access to the market. And its older-generation hardware also means performance is slow.

Dell Streak

PRICE From £299.18
OVERALL ★★★☆☆

The Streak is the only 5in tablet on the market, and it's very much a hybrid device. Its earpiece speaker and 3G connection let you hold it to your ear and use it as a phone, and its 5in screen is big enough for comfortable browsing.

It runs Android 2.2, but that's fine, since the phone OS feels more at home on a 5in screen than on larger devices. Dell's Stage UI skin gives it a tablet feel, too.

The problem is the niche it sits in is being squeezed: on one side by high-end smartphones such as Samsung's Galaxy S II and the Motorola Atrix, and on the other by powerful 7in tablets such as the HTC Flyer. It's pricey, too.

ViewSonic ViewPad 10s

PRICE From £286
OVERALL ★★★☆☆

There's very little difference between the ViewPad 10s and the Advent Vega. The chassis and internal hardware are near identical and, alas, that means it has the same dreadful screen. It runs an ugly version of Android 2.2, and also lacks access to the Android Market. The only thing in its favour is its 16GB of storage, but the price soon dampens any appeal that might bring. At £286, it's £86 dearer than the Vega, too.

Chapter 11

Google workshops

**Use Google to manage
your bookmarks online** 118

**Use Google Calendar's
advanced features** 121

**Display your photos
as a YouTube slideshow** 122

**Use Google Sites to
create a free family website** 124

Use Google to manage your bookmarks online

Your web browser seems like the obvious place to store your bookmarks. The only drawback is that if you need to use a different browser, your bookmarks won't be there. Syncing goes some way to solving this problem, but the best solution is to use an online bookmarking service that you can access from anywhere.

Our favourite is Google Bookmarks – a simple service that collects and organises your bookmarks as you browse the web. Your bookmarks are private by default, but easily accessible from your Google account. If you want to share them with others, you can convert them into Google Lists. This is a separate collection of bookmarks that can be made public or shared with individuals.

The best trick up Google Bookmarks' sleeve is that Google will highlight your links in standard search results, if it thinks they're relevant to the keywords you're searching for. So you don't even need to remember that you previously bookmarked something interesting to find it again.

ABOUT GOOGLE BOOKMARKS
Google Bookmarks can be found at www.google.com/bookmarks. To use the service, you need a Google account. If you don't already have one, you can get one for free – go to the link above and click 'Create an account now'.

1 Click 'Add bookmark'. 1 You can paste the name 2 and address 3 of a new bookmark in here if you wish, but it's quicker to use the bookmarklet. Drag the Google Bookmark button 4 up to the Bookmarks toolbar. 5

2 When you come across a site you like, click the Google Bookmark button. 1 A new window will open where you can edit the bookmark by changing its name 2 and address, 3 and adding labels 4 and descriptive notes. 5

3 To delete a bookmark, click the star next to its name. 1 Refresh the page and it'll be gone. To delete more than one bookmark at a time, tick the boxes by the ones you want to delete 2 and press the Delete button. 3

4 You can add places to your bookmarks directly from Google Maps. Use Search to locate the place you're after and click the place marker 1 to get more information. 2 Click the star 3 to transfer the place to your bookmarks.

5 Labels are useful for organisation. A label can consist of more than one word **1** and bookmarks can have more than one label (separated by commas). **2** To create a new label while you're bookmarking, type it into the Labels box. **3** Click 'Manage labels' **4** to rename **5** or remove **6** them.

6 To share bookmarks with others, convert them to lists. To make a list from existing bookmarks, select them by ticking the boxes **1** and click 'Copy to list'. **2** From the drop-down options, select an existing list to add to **3** or 'Create new list'. **4**

7 On the new list's page, you'll find the Lists bookmarklet. **1** Drag this to your browser toolbar, **2** and click it when you find a page to add to a list. Write in a title, **3** create or choose a list from the Select List button **4** and click Save. **5**

8 Lists don't have to be arranged alphabetically. Tick the box next to the item you want to move **1** and click Organize. **2** You can move items up and down, or create sections where you can group bookmarks. **3**

9 Click the Share button. **1** In the 'People with access' tab, **2** enter the email address of anyone you want to share a bookmark with. Alternatively, select the Visibility tab and choose from Public **3** or Private. **4** Click Save. **5**

10 You can also let people know about your lists using the email and social-networking buttons. **1** They can choose to follow the list **2** and receive a message when it's updated. You automatically follow your own lists.

Use Google Calendar's advanced features

If you've never got past creating events or adding birthdays in Google Calendar, you're only scratching the surface of its capabilities. Here, we look at some of its advanced features

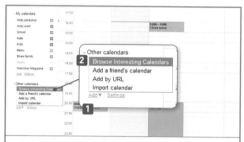

1 You can add public holidays, football team fixtures, contacts' birthdays and other significant events by clicking Add, **1** then Browse Interesting Calendars. **2** Select a calendar from the list (Holidays, Sports or More) and Subscribe. All relevant reminders will automatically appear on your calendar.

2 To add weather forecasts, click the cog, 'Calendar settings' and the General tab. Add your town or city in Location **1** and, in 'Show weather based on my location', choose Celsius or Fahrenheit. **2** Weather icons will now appear. Hover over them to show the temperature range.

3 To get notifications via text about scheduled events, go to the cog, 'Calendar settings', Mobile Setup tab. **1** Add your country, **2** mobile number **3** and a verification code **4** that will be sent to you. Compatible UK operators include 3, O2, Orange, T-Mobile and Vodafone. Charges may apply.

4 From Calendar Settings, click the Calendars tab **1** to change the way different calendars work. The Notifications link **2** lets you get reminders by default, via email or text message. You can also choose to Share, **3** Unsubscribe from **4** or Delete **5** calendars.

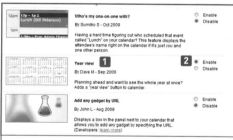

5 By default, Google Calendars can only be viewed by day, week, month or '4 days'. To see the whole year, go to the Labs tab in Calendar Settings. Scroll down to 'Year view', **1** click Enable **2** then Save. Year view will now be available from your homepage.

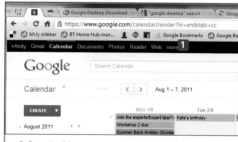

6 Google Chrome users can add the Google Calendar Checker extension (http://bit.ly/workshop1259), which places an icon on the toolbar **1** showing the length of time until your next meeting. Hover over the icon to display what the event is, and click it to go straight to your calendar.

Display your photos as a YouTube slideshow

Photos are great for capturing a fixed moment in time, but they rarely hold your attention in the same way that a video does. To make more of your snaps, YouTube offers a built-in app that lets you turn a collection of static photos and short video clips into a polished movie.

The Stupeflix Video Maker (www.youtube.com/create/stupeflix) is easy to use and doesn't require any specialised editing ability. Simply select a template, upload some images and rearrange them in sequence on the timeline. You can then add a soundtrack, some transitions and a couple of descriptive text slides. Click the button to save, and you can share the finished result online.

Like all YouTube submissions, Stupeflix creations are automatically made public, and shared by default with the world at large, but you can edit the privacy settings and limit viewing to selected friends and family if you prefer.

ABOUT STUPEFLIX

Free movies are restricted to a duration of one minute at a maximum resolution of 360p (640 x 360 pixels). You can upgrade to a Premium version for £3 (full length at 640 x 360 pixels with MP4 download enabled) or £6 (full length at 1,280 x 720 pixels).

1 Stupeflix Video Maker currently offers a selection of five template styles. **1** Click a style to find out more about it. When you've decided which one you want to use for your slideshow, select it and click the blue 'Make a video' button.

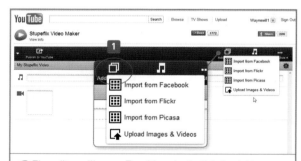

2 The editor will open. To add content, click the Add Images button. **1** You can import photos from Facebook, Flickr and Picasa, or upload images and videos from your hard disk. To select multiple items, hold down Ctrl or Shift.

3 You can select or import more photos while the first batch is uploading. Once processed, they'll be added to the timeline. **1** Reorder items by clicking and dragging, and use the slider **2** to zoom in or out.

4 Click the Add Audio button **1** to set background music. You can pick songs from Google's Music Lounge, select 'Text to Speech', or upload audio from your PC. Hover your mouse over a track and click Play to preview it. **2**

5 Drag the track you want to use to the Audio bar. **1** You can adjust its volume by clicking the down arrow at the end **2** and selecting Edit. Use the slider to set the volume, then click Done. **3** Click the up arrow **4** next to the Settings icon to close the music tray.

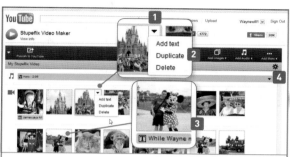

6 Hover your mouse over a thumbnail and a small down arrow will appear in the corner. **1** Click this to add a caption, duplicate the photo or delete it. **2** Captions **3** appear under the thumbnail and can be edited or deleted. Click the Settings button **4** to give your video a name.

EXPERT TIP
If you include too many photos in your slideshow, the video length will exceed the free one-minute limit. You can get around this by reducing the length of time that each photograph is displayed. Click Settings and change the pace from Normal to Fast.

7 You can add title slides and Google maps to a slideshow. Click the Add More button **1** and choose an option. When adding a map, you can type a place name. **2** Use the slider to zoom in or out. **3** Click Done **4** to add the slide.

8 To add a transition, click a thumbnail and select Custom Transitions. Stupeflix offers a choice of four styles. **1** Choose the one you want and click Done. **2** It's best to stick to the same transition style throughout your slideshow.

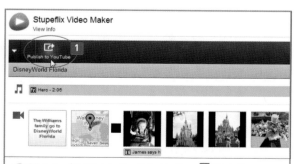

9 Click the 'Publish to YouTube' button. **1** Click Export and give Stupeflix permission to access your account. It will start to process your video and, after a brief wait, you'll be able to watch it and share it with friends.

10 Most of the video styles are customisable, but Celebrate has a more rigid structure. It has an audio track (Fanciful, **1** but you can change this) and the template follows a set order. **2** Double-click a text slide to edit it. **3**

Use Google Sites to create a free family website

It seems that everyone's got a website nowadays, from families to schools and book clubs. The idea of creating a site of your own sounds great, but can be daunting if you don't know where to start or how to manage it. As with most web-related tasks, Google provides an easy way to create professional-looking sites. Using Google Sites (https://sites.google.com), you can make your site as complicated or as simple as you like, and you can keep it private or share it with the world. There's even the option of letting other people help you edit and manage the content. It's a perfect way to create an online hub to share news and photos with family, show off a hobby or just simply have fun.

Google Sites has a wide range of templates to get you started. You can choose from lots of designs and customise the colour schemes before you start and, once the site is up and running, you can tweak the layout to suit your tastes. You don't need any design skills – Google Sites makes it easy to get an attractive-looking site onto the web with very little fuss.

> **ABOUT GOOGLE SITES**
> You need to have a Google account to set up a Google Site. If you don't already have one, go to the Google homepage to set up a free account. The free web-design application works within your browser.

1 To get started, choose a template **1** and a theme **2** from the list of popular layouts. Then give your site a name. **3** Common templates and themes are offered or you can browse the gallery **4** for more options.

2 Set who can see your site by going to 'More actions' **1** and choosing 'Share this site'. You can then change permissions, **2** share it on social networks **3** or email the link. **4**

3 When using a template, default images and text can be replaced. To edit any page on your site, click 'Edit page'. **1** This will open the Editor screen where you can insert photos, documents and tables, or adjust the layout.

4 To edit default boxes, click them to bring an Options menu up. **1** You can change the size **2** or delete the item by selecting Remove. **3** To replace elements, click Insert **4** and choose a replacement item from the list.

5 To create a profile for family members, exit the Editor screen, go to 'Family profiles' on the sidebar and click 'Create page'. Choose 'Profile page', **1** give your page a name **2** and select 'Put page under Family profiles'. **3** You can then overwrite the boxes and text.

6 Share your news using blog posts. Click 'Family blog' **1** from the sidebar then 'New post'. Insert any text or images as in Step 3. To publish, click Save **2** or to edit later, click 'Save as draft' in the top-right corner. All new posts appear on the homepage automatically.

EXPERT TIP
To share or post a slideshow on other sites as a taster for what's on your site, click the Picasa symbol in the bottom right of the slideshow box. Then click 'Get your own'. This will give you the embed code for this album. This code can be copied into your Facebook or MySpace account, other websites or a blog. You can let others add images by emailing the URL and setting each addressee as 'Can edit'.

7 To replace the default calendar, open the Editor screen. Click 'Family calendar' **1**, go to the Insert menu **2** and choose Calendar. Any calendars already created will show in the list. Choose one, **3** click Select **4** then Save.

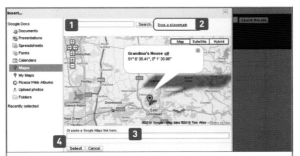

8 To add a map featuring everyone's address, click the Insert menu from the Editor screen and choose Map. Search for an address, **1** then select 'Drop a placemark' **2** or paste a Google Maps link. **3** Click Select, **4** then Save.

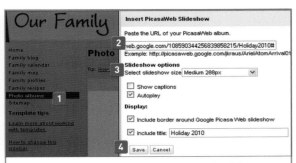

9 To share photo albums, you'll need to upload them to PicasaWeb Albums. Once uploaded, click 'Photo albums'. **1** Go to Insert, then 'PicasaWeb slideshow'. Paste the URL, **2** set your slideshow options, **3** then Save. **4**

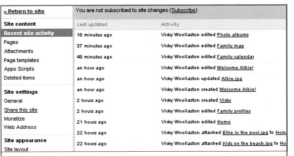

10 You can change who you share the site with or its layout, theme, name and other settings by clicking 'More actions', then 'Manage site' from the viewing screen.

Google A-Z

Here's everything Google does in a handy list A-Z list

+1 Button www.google.com/+1
20 Things I Learned www.20thingsilearned.com
3D Warehouse http://sketchup.google.com/3dwarehouse

A

A Google a Day www.agoogleaday.com
Accounts www.google.com/accounts
AdSense www.google.com/adsense
Alerts http://alerts.google.com
Analytics www.google.com/analytics
Android www.android.com
Android Developers http://developer.android.com
Android Market https://market.android.com
App Engine http://appengine.google.com
App Inventor http://appinventor.googlelabs.com
Art Project www.googleartproject.com

B

Blog http://googleblog.blogspot.com
Blogger www.blogger.com
Bookmarks http://bookmarks.google.com
Books http://books.google.com
Buzz http://buzz.google.com

C

Calendar http://calendar.google.com
Chart API http://code.google.com/apis/chart
Checkout http://checkout.google.com
Chrome http://chrome.google.com
Chrome Experiments www.chromeexperiments.com
Chrome OS www.google.com/chromeos
Chrome Web Store http://chrome.google.com/webstore
Chromium www.chromium.org/Home
Chromium OS www.chromium.org/chromium-os
Cloud Connect for Microsoft Office http://tools.google.com/dlpage/cloudconnect
Cloud Print www.google.com/cloudprint
Code http://code.google.com
Code University http://code.google.com/edu
Codesearch www.google.com/codesearch
Compare UK Mortgages https://www.google.com/comparisonads/ukmortgage

Correlate www.google.com/trends/correlate
Crisis Response www.google.com/crisisresponse
Custom Search Engine www.google.com/cse

D

Docs http://docs.google.com
Doodles http://www.google.com/logos
DoubleClick www.google.com/doubleclick

E

Earth http://earth.google.com
Earth Engine www.google.org/earthengine
Earth Outreach http://earth.google.com/outreach
eBooks http://ebooks.google.com
Election Center http://electioncenter.googlelabs.com

F

Fastflip http://fastflip.googlelabs.com
Feedburner http://feedburner.google.com
Finance http://finance.google.com
For Educators www.google.com/educators
Friend Connect www.google.com/friendconnect
Fusion Tables www.google.com/fusiontables

G

Gmail www.gmail.com
Go http://golang.org
Goggles www.google.com/mobile/goggles
Goobuntu http://en.wikipedia.org/wiki/Goobuntu
Google www.google.com
Google Apps for EDU www.google.com/a/help/intl/en/edu
Groups http://groups.google.com

I

iGoogle www.google.com/ig
Image Chart Editor http://imagecharteditor.appspot.com
Images http://images.google.com
Insights www.google.com/insights/search
Instant Search http://instant.google.com

J

Jobs http://jobs.google.com

K

Keyword Tool www.googlekeywordtool.com
Knol http://knol.google.com

L

Latitude http://latitude.google.com
Listen http://listen.googlelabs.com
Logos www.google.com/logos
Lunar X Prize www.googlelunarxprize.org

M

Map Maker http://mapmaker.google.com
Maps http://maps.google.com
Mobile www.google.com/mobile
Moderator www.google.com/moderator
Music http://music.google.com

N

New products www.google.com/newproducts
News http://news.google.com

O

Offers www.google.com/offers
One Pass www.google.com/onepass
Orkut www.orkut.com

P

Phone gallery www.google.com/phone
Picasa http://picasa.google.com
Places http://places.google.com
Plus http://plus.google.com
Products http://products.google.com
Profiles http://profiles.google.com
Public Data Explorer http://publicdata.google.com

Q

Quick Search Box www.google.com/quicksearchbox (Mac only)

R

Reader http://reader.google.com
Reader Play www.google.com/reader/play

ReCAPTCHA www.google.com/recaptcha
Related www.google.com/related

S

Scholar http://scholar.google.com
Search Stories www.youtube.com/user/SearchStories
Secure Search www.google.com
Shared Spaces http://sharedspaces.googlelabs.com
Sitemap www.google.com/sitemap.xml
Sites http://sites.google.com
SketchUp http://sketchup.google.com
Sky http://sky.google.com
Store www.googlestore.com
Street View http://maps.google.com/help/maps/streetview

T

Talk http://talk.google.com
Tasks http://mail.google.com/mail/help/tasks
Teach Parents Tech www.teachparentstech.org
Toolbar http://toolbar.google.com
Translate http://translate.google.com
Trends http://trends.google.com
TV www.google.com/tv

U

URL Shortener http://goo.gl

V

Video http://video.google.com
Voice http://voice.google.com

W

Wallet www.google.com/wallet
Web History www.google.com/history
Webmaster Central www.google.com/webmasters
Website Optimizer www.google.com/websiteoptimizer

Y

YouTube www.youtube.com

Z

Zeitgeist www.google.com/intl/en/press/zeitgeist

And finally...

G⬤⬤gle

GAMES

We reveal our favourite Google time wasters

Chrome FastBall
www.youtube.com/user/chromefastball
The YouTube-based game Chrome FastBall invites you to race across the internet, completing challenges that test your knowledge of languages, facts and even public transport using Google tools. The game involves five timed challenges – as you complete each level you move a ball bearing through an obstacle course, and skipping questions incurs a 60-second penalty. You can see how your surfing skills compare on a global leader board of around 160,000 players. Despite the name, Chrome FastBall also works in other web browsers.

Google Pac-Man
www.google.com/pacman
Google's 30th anniversary Pac-Man doodle proved so popular in 2010, it's now available permanently. Guide Pac-Man around a Google-logo maze using the arrow keys, scoffing 'pac-dots' and avoiding ghosts. Eating large dots makes the ghosts edible for a short time while collecting all the dots moves you to the next level. Also, if you click the Insert Coins button twice, the game switches to two-player mode, with both Pac-Man and Ms Pac-Man – she is controlled using the W, A, S and D keys.

Google Image Quiz
www.gamesforthebrain.com/game/imagequiz
Like an online version of a pub-quiz picture round, this time waster asks you to identify images taken from Google's library. You get three guesses each round and lose points for incorrect answers.

Streetview Zombie Apocalypse
http://wonder-tonic.com/zombie
This addictive game takes you into a location of your choice where you have to escape a zombie invasion. Stay alive for as long as possible by running through streets using the onscreen navigation tools in Street View.

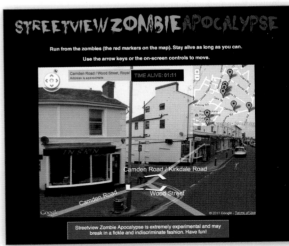